OECD Reviews on Local Job Creation

Employment and Skills Strategies in Flanders, Belgium

This work is published on the responsibility of the Secretary-General of the OECD. The opinions expressed and arguments employed herein do not necessarily reflect the official views of the Organisation or of the governments of its member countries.

This document and any map included herein are without prejudice to the status of or sovereignty over any territory, to the delimitation of international frontiers and boundaries and to the name of any territory, city or area.

Please cite this publication as:
OECD (2015), *Employment and Skills Strategies in Flanders, Belgium*, OECD Reviews on Local Job Creation, OECD Publishing.
http://dx.doi.org/10.1787/9789264228740-en

ISBN 978-92-64-22798-9 (print)
ISBN 978-92-64-22874-0 (PDF)

Series: OECD Reviews on Local Job Creation
ISSN 2311-2328 (print)
ISSN 2311-2336 (online)

The statistical data for Israel are supplied by and under the responsibility of the relevant Israeli authorities. The use of such data by the OECD is without prejudice to the status of the Golan Heights, East Jerusalem and Israeli settlements in the West Bank under the terms of international law.

Photo credits: © Andy Dean Photography/Shutterstock.com; © ZaZa Studio/Shutterstock.com.

Corrigenda to OECD publications may be found on line at: *www.oecd.org/publishing/corrigenda*.

Preface

Across the OECD, policy makers are grappling with a critical question: how to create jobs? The recent financial crisis and economic downturn has had serious consequences across most OECD countries, with rising unemployment rates and jobs being lost across many sectors. Indeed, for some countries, the effects of the downturn are continuing, if not amplifying. Shrinking public budgets in some countries also mean that policy makers must now do more with less. In this context, it is necessary to think laterally about how actions in one area, such as employment and training, can have simultaneous benefits in others, such as creating new jobs and better supporting labour market inclusion.

Over recent years, the work of the OECD LEED Programme on *Designing Local Skills Strategies*, *Building Flexibility and Accountability into Local Employment Services*, *Breaking out of Policy Silos*, *Leveraging Training and Skills Development in SMEs*, and *Skills for Competitiveness* has demonstrated that local strategies to boost skills and job creation require the participation of many different actors across employment, training, economic development, and social welfare portfolios. Employers, unions and the non-profit sector are also key partners in ensuring that education and training programmes provide the skills needed in the labour markets of today and the future.

The *OECD Reviews on Local Job Creation* deliver evidence-based and practical recommendations on how to better support employment and economic development at the local level. This report builds on sub-national data analysis and consultations at the regional level and with local stakeholders in two case study areas. It provides a comparative framework to understand the role of the local level in contributing to more and better quality jobs. The report can help regional and local policy makers in Flanders, Belgium build effective and sustainable partnerships at the local level, which join-up efforts and achieve stronger outcomes across employment, training, and economic development policies. Co-ordinated policies can help workers find suitable jobs, while also stimulating entrepreneurship and productivity, which increases the quality of life and prosperity within a community as well as throughout the country.

I would like to warmly thank the Flemish Department of Work and the Social Economy for their active participation and support of the study.

Sergio Arzeni,

Director, OECD Centre for Entrepreneurship,
SMEs and Local Development

Acknowledgments

This report has been prepared under the Local Economic and Employment Development (LEED) Programme of the Organisation for Economic Co-operation and Development (OECD) as part of a project undertaken in co-operation with the Flemish Department of Work and the Social Economy. The review is part of the programme of work of the OECD LEED Division under the leadership of Sylvain Giguère.

The principal authors are Katleen De Rick (HIVA – Research Institute for Work and Society, KU Leuven) and Jonathan Barr (Policy Analyst, OECD). Francesca Froy (Senior Policy Analysts, OECD) provided valuable comments on the report. Thanks also go to Michela Meghnagi and Nikolett Kis for their work the data analysis, as well as François Iglesias, Malika Taberkane and other colleagues in the OECD LEED Programme for their assistance with this report and project.

The authors would also like to acknowledge the valuable contributions of Lars Nikalsson (Linkping University, Sweden) and Steve Johnson (Hull University, the United Kingdom) for their participation in the OECD study visit and comments on this report.

Special thanks should be also given to the representatives at the local and regional level who participated in meetings and provided documentation and comments critical to the production of this report.

Table of contents

Acronyms and abbreviations 7

Executive summary 9

Reader's guide 12

Chapter 1. Policy context for employment and skills in Flanders, Belgium 15
- Economic and labour market trends 16
- Worrying trends in job creation 17
- The supply of skills 18
- Mapping the institutional framework for employment and skills policies 19
- Active labour market policies in Flanders 21
- Other actors involved with employment and skills policies at the local level 21
- The importance of collective bargaining and social dialogue in Flanders 22
- Vocational education and training system (VET) 23
- References 25

Chapter 2. Overview of the Flanders, Belgium case study areas 27
- Overview of the case study areas 28
- City of Antwerp 28
- Limburg 29
- Comparison across the case study areas 30
- Balance between skills supply and demand at the sub-national level 32
- Results from the data mapping exercise 34
- References 34

Chapter 3. Local job creation dashboard findings in Flanders, Belgium 35
- Results from the dashboard 36
- Theme 1: Better aligning policy and programmes to local economic development 37
- Theme 2: Adding value through skills 44
- Theme 3: Targeting policy to local employment sectors and investing in quality jobs 49
- Theme 4: Being inclusive 54
- References 59

Chapter 4. Towards an action plan for jobs in Flanders, Belgium: Recommendations and best practices 61
- Better aligning programmes and policies to local economic development 62
- Adding value through skills 65

Targeting policy to local employment sectors and investing in quality jobs 73
Being inclusive 77
References 79

Table

2.1. Employment by economic activity, 2012 31

Figures

1.1. GDP growth in Belgium compared to the EU average, 2004-13 16
1.2. Unemployment rates in Belgium compared to the EU average, 2004-13 17
1.3. Youth unemployment in Belgium compared to the EU average, 2005-13 18
1.4. Persons aged 25-64 with tertiary education attainment, Flemish regions, 2004-13 19
1.5. OECD Survey of Adult Skills, results across regions in Flanders 20
2.1. Map of Antwerp 28
2.2. Map of the Limburg region 29
2.3. Understanding the relationship between skills supply and demand 32
2.4. Skills supply and demand in Belgium, TL2 regions, 2010 33
2.5. Skills supply and demand in Belgium, TL3 regions, 2001 33
2.6. Skills supply and demand in Belgium, TL3 regions, 2010 34
3.1. Local Job Creation Dashboard – Flanders 36
3.2. Local Job Creation Dashboard: Better aligning policies and programmes to local economic development 37
3.3. Local job creation dashboard: Adding value through skills 44
3.4. Local job creation dashboard – Targeting policy to local employment sectors and investing in quality jobs 50
3.5. Local Job Creation Dashboard – Being inclusive 54

Acronyms and abbreviations

ALMP	Active labour market programmes
ERSVs	Recognized regional partnerships (*erkend regionaal samenwerkingsverband)*
ERDF	European regional development funds
EU	European Union
ESF	European social fund
LEED	Local Economic and Employment Development
NEET	Not in education, employment or training
OCMW	Public social welfare centre (*Openbare Centra voor Maatschappelijk Welzijn*)
OECD	Organisation of Economic Co-operation and Development
PES	Public Employment Service
PIAAC	Programme for the International Assessment of Adult Competencies
PWA	Local employment agencies (*Plaatselijk Werkgelegenheidsagentschap)*
RESOC	Regional Economic and Social Consultation Committee (*Regionaal Economisch en Sociaal Overlegcomité)*
RTC	Regional technological centres
SALK	Strategic Action Plan Limburg (*Strategisch Actieplan Limburg in't Kwadraat*)
SERV	Flemish Socio-Economical Council (*Sociaal-Economische Raad van Vlaanderen)*
SERR	Socio-Economic Council of the Region (*Sociaal-economische raad van de region)*
SME	Small and medium sized enterprise
TL	Territorial level
VDAB	Flemish Public Employment Service
VESOC	Flemish Economic Social Consultation Committee (*Vlaams Economisch Sociaal Overlegcomité)*
VET	Vocational education and training
VLOR	Flemish Education Council (*Vlaamse Onderwijsraad)*

Executive summary

Flanders emerged from the global financial crisis in a relatively healthy position with stable unemployment levels compared to the OECD average. However, certain groups of individuals, such as youth and older workers face significant barriers to successful labour force participation. Creating quality jobs and developing relevant skills will be an important priority to continue growing the economy.

The OECD Local Economic and Employment Development Programme (LEED) has developed an international comparative project to examine the capacity of local employment services and training providers to contribute to a long-term strategy which strengthens the resiliency of the local economy, increases skills levels and improves job quality. In Flanders, the review has looked at the range of institutions and bodies involved in employment and skills policies. In-depth work was undertaken in the Antwerp and Limburg regions.

It is encouraging that VDAB (the agency for public employment services) has moved towards a flexible management model, however more needs to be done to explore how to combine actions locally across employment, skills, and economic development portfolios. Another important policy imperative is to develop data sharing platforms across local providers and organisations, which can be used to provide actionable and real time information on gaps in the supply and demand of skills. By sharing information across organisations, local actors can ensure they are successfully meeting the needs of employers, who are a critical source of job creation.

Efforts to reduce skills mismatches and shortages require stronger engagement with employers in the facilitation of workplace training opportunities. While there are good examples of collaboration through the sectoral training funds, more can be done to articulate the benefits of training to employers and alert them to the opportunities available through these programmes. Employers and workers have a joint role to play in this by supporting a culture of workplace learning. It is important to build on good bottom up collaboration and networks that already exist.

While there are some initiatives undertaken at the local level, particularly in the Limburg region, skills utilisation efforts are not comprehensively supported across Flanders. The Flemish government should encourage closer working with employers to stimulate demand side initiatives under a mantra of Corporate Social Responsibility, which recognises the public and private benefits of encouraging and promoting quality jobs. The Talent Houses in Antwerp are working well to match skills to certain sectors; however, much of their focus is on supply side initiatives. There is an opportunity for them to shift efforts towards how to stimulate the demand for skills, which would create higher quality jobs and thereby attract higher skilled people into the city and region, which has broader economic development benefits.

To ensure that the supply of skills adequately meets labour market demand, it is important to strengthen the linkages between the education system and employment, and training agencies. Schools should work more closely with the public employment service and vocational education system to create clearer, simpler and more recognised pathways into training as well as the labour market. In particular, it is important that more out-reach is conducted by VDAB with secondary schools to ensure that youth at-risk can be identified early and adequate supports and interventions can be put in place to reduce early school leavers and the number of NEETs. At the local level, addressing youth unemployment is a clear policy priority in both Antwerp and Limburg. A number of comprehensive programmes and policies have been put in place, which aim to provide work experience opportunities and develop long-term labour market attachment.

Another critical lever in stimulating job creation locally is creating a culture of entrepreneurship. This is particularly important for local areas, which are experiencing structural adjustments, such as the Limburg region, where the Ford factory is set to close, resulting in significant direct and indirect job losses for the community. Entrepreneurship skills can assist individuals in developing successful businesses and creating jobs. Therefore, the vocational and higher education system should ensure that course curriculum includes an adequate focus on building these types of skills.

Key recommendations

Better aligning programmes and policies to local economic development

- Build on the high level of flexibility within employment services and continue to build partnerships and horizontal accountability mechanisms, which promote growth and employment. This can be done by identifying the best collaboration models which have led to strong policy integration and co-ordination.
- Continue to collect and share information and data about "what works" locally, including effective approaches to respond to the hiring needs of employers.

Adding value through skills

- Proceed with the reform of the apprenticeship system to make it a more attractive vocational educational pathway and foster more opportunities for work-based training.
- Promote stronger engagement with employers in the design and implementation of employment and training programmes to create a culture of lifelong learning. Encourage network formation among employers who can take a lead role in the delivery of employment and skills policies.
- Ensure career guidance and information systems are well-targeted to youth and individuals who are unemployed or at-risk of adjustment to support labour force attachment, as well as career progression and advancement.

Targeting policy to local employment sectors and investing in quality jobs

- Stimulate overall productivity and job quality through policies which promote the better utilisation of skills. Encourage the Talent Houses to focus on working with employers to stimulate overall demand for skills to boost local growth and competiveness.
- Build stronger entrepreneurship skills for youth and adults to stimulate overall demand and job creation. This can be done by promoting entrepreneurship as a viable career

option and providing comprehensive support and tools to individuals to help them start their own business.

Being inclusive

- Strengthen linkages between the education system and employment, and training agencies to reduce youth drop-outs. Continue to target early-school leavers and provide follow-up support while examining ways of involving youth more in programme design and delivery.

Reader's guide

The *Local Job Creation* project involves a series of country reviews in Australia, Belgium (Flanders), Canada (Ontario and Quebec), Czech Republic, France, Ireland, Israel, Italy (Autonomous Province of Trento), Korea, Sweden, the United Kingdom and the United States (California and Michigan). The key stages of each review are summarised in Box 1.

Box 1. **Summary of the OECD LEED Local Job Creation Project Methodology**

- Analyse available data to understand the key labour market challenges facing the country in the context of the economic recovery and apply an OECD LEED diagnostic tool which seeks to assess the balance between the supply and demand for skills at the local level.
- Map the current policy framework for local job creation in the country.
- Apply the local Job Creation Dashboard, developed by the OECD LEED Programme (Froy et al., 2010) to measure the relative strengths and weaknesses of local employment and training agencies to contribute to job creation.
- Conduct an OECD study visit, where local and national roundtables with a diverse range of stakeholders are held to discuss the results and refine the findings and recommendations.
- Contribute to policy development in the reviewed country by proposing policy options to overcome barriers, illustrated by selected good practice initiatives from other OECD countries.

While the economic crisis is the current focus of policy-makers, there is a need for both short-term and longer-term actions to ensure sustainable economic growth. In response to this issue, the OECD LEED Programme has developed a set of thematic areas on which local stakeholders and employment and training agencies can focus to build sustainable growth at the local level. These include:

1. **Better aligning policies and programmes to local economic development challenges and opportunities;**
2. **Adding value through skills:** Creating an adaptable skilled labour force and supporting employment progression and skills upgrading;
3. **Targeting policy to local employment sectors and investing in quality jobs:** including gearing education and training to emerging local growth sectors and responding to global trends, while working with employers on skills utilisation and productivity; and,
4. **Being inclusive** to ensure that all actual and potential members of the labour force can contribute to future economic growth.

Local Job Creation Dashboard

As part of the Local Job Creation Project, the LEED Programme has drawn on its previous research to develop a set of best practice priorities in each thematic area, which is used to assess local practice through the local Job Creation Dashboard (see Box 2). The dashboard enables national and local policy-makers to gain a stronger overview of the strengths and weaknesses of the current policy framework, whilst better prioritising future actions and resources. A value between 1 (low) to 5 (high) is assigned to each of the four priority areas corresponding to the relative strengths and weaknesses of local policy approaches based on LEED research and best practices in other OECD countries.

Box 2. **Local Job Creation Dashboard**

Better aligning policies and programmes to local economic development

1.1. Flexibility in the delivery of employment and vocational training policies

1.2. Capacities within employment and VET sectors

1.3. Policy co-ordination, policy integration and co-operation with other sectors

1.4. Evidence based policy making

Adding value through skills

2.1. Flexible training open to all in a broad range of sectors

2.2. Working with employers on training

2.3. Matching people to jobs and facilitating progression

2.4. Joined up approaches to skills

Targeting policy to local employment sectors and investing in quality jobs

3.1. Relevance of provision to important local employment sectors and global trends and challenges

3.2. Working with employers on skills utilisation and productivity

3.3. Promotion of skills for entrepreneurship

3.4. Promoting quality jobs through local economic development

Being inclusive

4.1. Employment and training programmes geared to local "at-risk" groups

4.2. Childcare and family friendly policies to support women's participation in employment

4.3. Tackling youth unemployment

4.4. Openness to immigration

The approach for Flanders

This study has looked at the range of institutions and bodies involved in workforce and skills development in Flanders, Belgium. In-depth field work focused on two case study regions: Antwerp and Limburg.

In January 2014, two local roundtables were held in each of the case study areas and a national roundtable was held to discuss the findings and recommendations. These meetings brought together a range of regional and local stakeholders, including relevant department officials in the fields of employment, economic development, and training; employers; and other local community and social development organisations.

References

Froy, F., S. Giguère and E. Travkina (2010), *Local Job Creation: Project Methodology*, *www.oecd.org/cfe/leed/Local%20Job%20Creation%20Methodology_27%20February.pdf*.

Chapter 1

Policy context for employment and skills in Flanders, Belgium

The Belgian economy remained relatively resilient through the recent economic crisis. In particular, Flanders has one of the lowest unemployment rates across the three main regions in the country. However, unemployment among youth remains stubbornly high and will be a significant policy challenge moving forward. This chapter provides an overview of the employment and skills system in Flanders and describes the key institutional actors at the national, regional, and local level.

Economic and labour market trends

While the economic crisis had an impact on the Belgian economy, it was relatively resilient when compared to other countries in the European Union. While there was a significant contraction of GDP between 2008-2010, it was not as dramatic as the EU28 average (see Figure 1.1). Since, 2008, Belgium continues to perform slightly better than the EU average. According to the latest *OECD Economic Survey of Belgium*, the economy experienced a small contraction in 2012 due to continued weak growth in real disposable income, fiscal consolidation and weakening growth in Europe and the world (OECD, 2012).

Figure 1.1. **GDP growth in Belgium compared to the EU average, 2004-13**

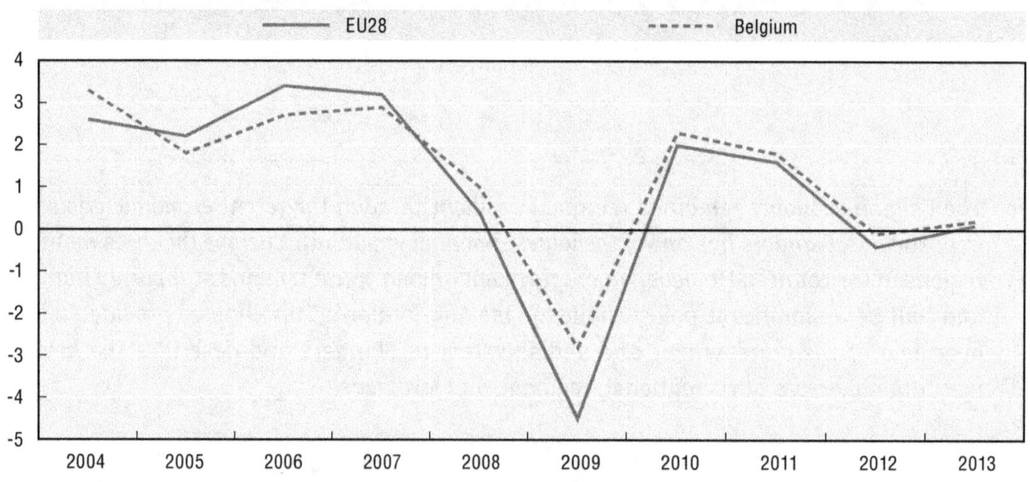

Source: Eurostat, *http://ec.europa.eu/eurostat/tgm/table.do?tab=table&init=1&plugin=1&language=en&pcode=tec00115.*

These factors were reflected in a contraction of household consumption and housing investment, as well as a sharp slowing of exports (OECD, 2013a). A slow recovery is expected in 2015 as world trade growth is gathering speed and domestic demand is being stimulated by supportive euro-area monetary policy. The performance of the labour market has been relatively good. During the crisis, the unemployment rate increased less than in other European countries reflecting widespread labour hoarding, in part through the large use of reduced work time schemes (see Figure 1.2) (OECD, 2013a).

Despite the continuous increase of the unemployment rates in all 3 regions in Belgium since 2011, the national average unemployment rate of 8.4% in 2013 was still lower than the EU-28 average of 10.8% Belgium has the fourth highest level of regional variation in the unemployment in 2012 among OECD countries after Spain, Italy, and the Slovak Republic (OECD, 2014a). Regional variation increased in 2013 as the unemployment rate of the Brussels Capital Region increased by nearly 2% in one year. Unemployment has remained lowest in Flanders (5% in 2013), whereas Brussels had an unemployment rate well above the EU average (almost 19.2% in 2013). The unemployment rate for Wallonia was close to the

Figure 1.2. **Unemployment rates in Belgium compared to the EU average, 2004-13**

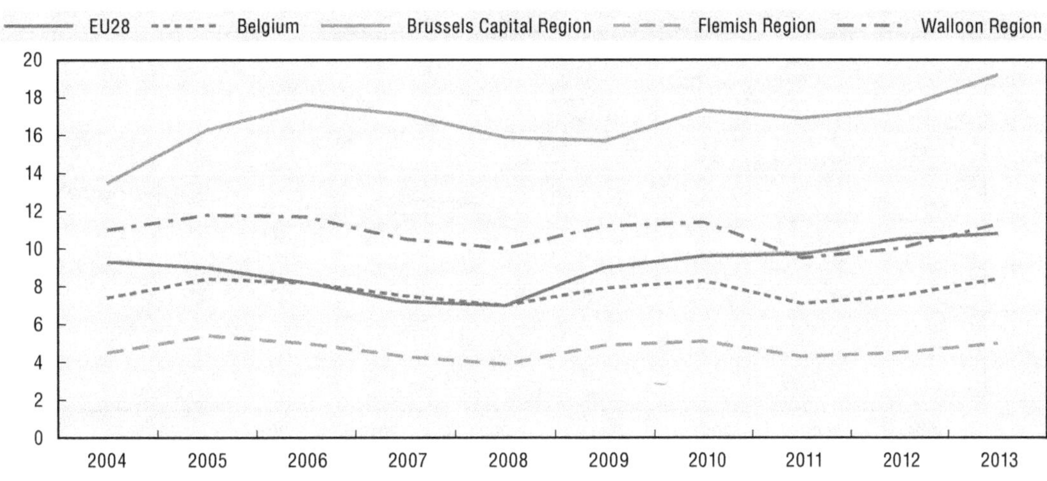

Source: Eurostat, *http://appsso.eurostat.ec.europa.eu/nui/show.do?dataset=lfst_r_lfu3rt&lang=en.*

EU28 at 11.3% in 2013. Among Flemish provinces, Antwerp and Limburg are the regions with higher unemployment rates. Between 2007 and 2013, unemployment increased in Antwerp, Flemish Brabant, and West Flanders, while Limburg and East Flanders saw mild decreases.

The OECD's 2013 *Economic Survey of Belgium* notes that longstanding structural labour market problems remain, such as high structural unemployment, low employment rates for younger and older workers and for low-skilled immigrants; as well as large labour market mismatches (OECD, 2013a). Labour market mismatches are roughly similar to 2007, before the crisis began. Vacancies are mostly for skilled workers but 80% of job-seekers are low or medium skilled workers, and about half are long-term unemployed (Zimmer, 2012). In Flanders, a large number of jobs remain vacant in 162 identified positions with particular shortages in IT engineers and nurses. Eighty-eight of these professions require a diploma above secondary education but below a bachelor's degree (Flemish Department Education and Training, 2013).

Youth have been particularly impacted by the crisis, including in certain regions in Belgium. The youth unemployment rate in Belgium reached 23.7% in 2013, the highest level in the last 10 years and for the first time since 2010 slightly higher than the EU average (see Figure 1.3). Regional variation is also significant; in the Brussels Capital region, the rate is 39.9%, which is slightly above the post crisis rate in 2010. Youth unemployment increased in the Walloon region by nearly 6 percentage points in one year reaching 33% in 2013. In the Flemish region, it was 17% in 2013 which was also the highest rate in the last decade even though this is still well below the EU average. The share of Belgian youth (aged 15-24) who are not employed and not in education or training (NEET) was 12% in 2013 which is lower than the OECD average (OECD, 2014b).

Worrying trends in job creation

Work undertaken by DynaM analysis points to some worrying concerns in job creation trends across Belgium. Recent figures show that at no time in the last ten years have fewer jobs been created in the labour market than during the most recent crisis period (2011-13) (Bulté and Struyven, 2013). The recent crisis (2011-13) has brought a worrying degree of low job creation compared to the first period of the crisis from 2008-09 where there was an even

Figure 1.3. **Youth unemployment in Belgium compared to the EU average, 2005-13**

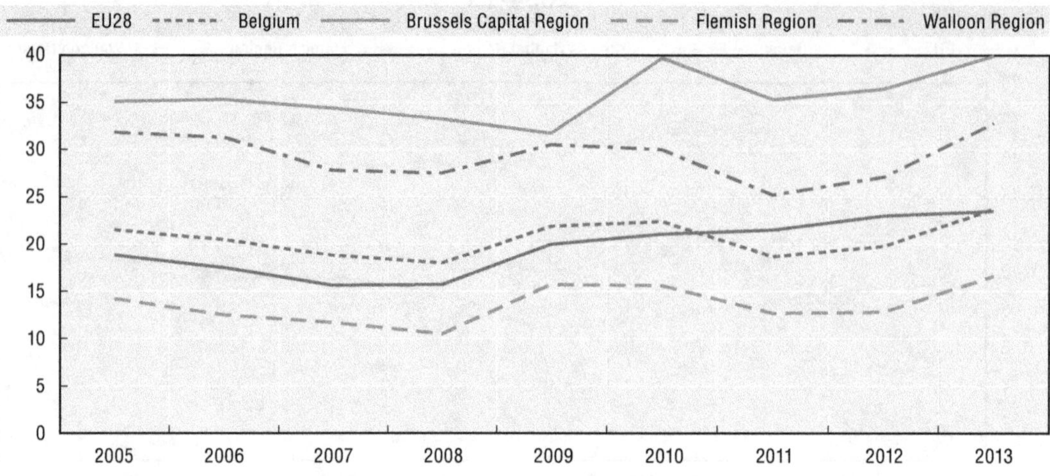

Source: Eurostat, *http://appsso.eurostat.ec.europa.eu/nui/show.do?dataset=lfst_r_lfe2emprt&lang=en.*

process of "creative destruction" (e.g. while many jobs were lost, new ones were being created at the same time).

Between June 2011 and June 2012, there was a net change of -14 500 jobs (-.04%) with 187 000 jobs created but 201 500 jobs destroyed. The jobs that were created were within existing companies (not by new companies). The loss of jobs continued in 2012 with a net change in job creation of -0.7% meaning more jobs were destroyed than created. In particular, jobs in the public sector and education are disappearing faster than they are being created, carrying significant implications for both the case study areas that are analysed in-depth as part of this study. Unfortunately, job creation data is not available at a lower disaggregation within Belgium to compare regions within Flanders.

The supply of skills

In 2011, almost three of four Belgians had at least an upper secondary education: 71% of 25-64 year-olds compared to the OECD average of 75% (OECD, 2013b). 82% of 25-34 year olds have at least an upper-secondary education equal to the OECD average. Within the region of Flanders, the province of Flemish Brabant has a significantly higher percentage of population with tertiary education than the other four provinces. It was 44.3% in 2013 which compares to a regional average of 35.7%. Limburg shows the lowest rate at 28.7% in 2013. All five provinces show an average growth in the last decade, among them West Flanders shows the most rapid increase of population with tertiary education, where the rate grew by 8 percentage points between 2004 and 2013.

As part of its Programme for the International Assessment of Adult Competencies (PIAAC), the OECD collects and analyses data that assist governments in assessing, monitoring and analysing the level and distribution of skills among their adult populations as well as the utilisation of skills in different contexts. It measures the key cognitive and workplace skills needed for individuals to participate in society and for economies to prosper.

Looking at the results from the PIAAC survey, adults in Flanders show above average proficiency in literacy and numeracy and average proficiency in problem solving in technology-rich environments compared with other countries who participated in the survey (OECD, 2013c). Young adults in Flanders (16-24 years old) have above average

Figure 1.4. **Persons aged 25-64 with tertiary education attainment, Flemish regions, 2004-13**

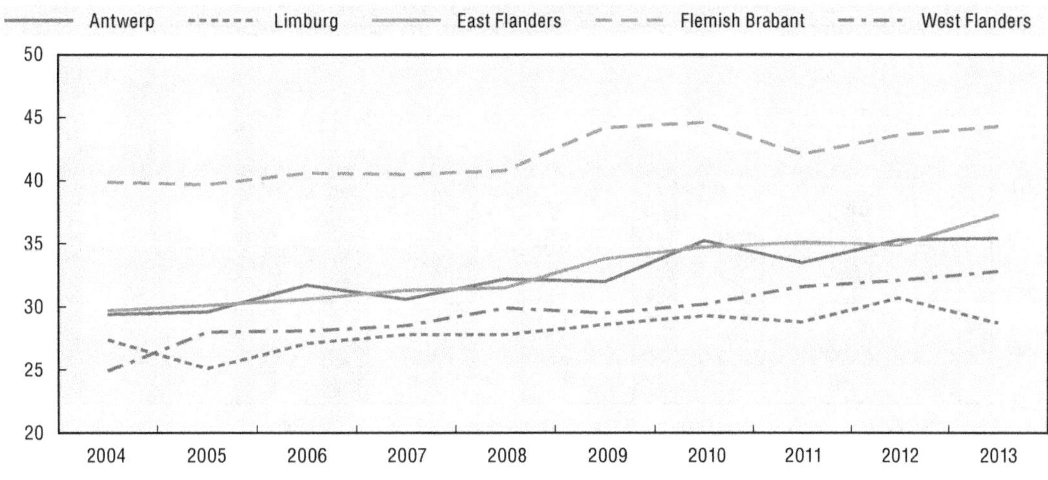

Source: Eurostat, *http://ec.europa.eu/eurostat/tgm/table.do?tab=table&init=1&language=en&pcode=tgs00109&plugin=1.*

proficiency in literacy, numeracy, and problem solving in technology rich environments on average compared with other OECD countries (OECD, 2013c).

For example, some 12.4% of adults in Flanders (aged 16-65) attain the two highest levels of proficiency in literacy (Level 4 or 5) compared with the average of 11.8% of adults in all participating countries. Some 14.0% of adults in Flanders attain only Level 1 or below in literacy proficiency (compared with the average of 15.5%) and 13.4% attain Level 1 or below in numeracy (compared with the average of 19.0%) (OECD, 2013c). Some 82.1% of adults in Flanders scoring at Level 4/5 in literacy are employed compared to only 55% of those scoring at or below Level 1, which demonstrates the strong impact that literacy and numeracy have on labour market outcomes (OECD, 2013c). The rate of inactivity (16.3%) among highly proficient (Level 4/5) adults in Flanders is slightly below the average (17.1%) among participating countries (OECD, 2013c).

Proficiency in literacy, numeracy, and problem solving differs significant when looking at the results at the regional level in Flanders (see Figure 1.5). Adults in Flemish-Brabant show relatively higher levels of literacy, numeracy, and problem solving skills. Antwerp also has relatively high scores especially in numeracy and problem solving. The region of Limburg shows a relatively lower level of proficiency in literacy and problem solving skills when compared to other regions in Flanders. Numeracy was the lowest in East Flanders. Mobility may partly explain the strong regional variations with more proficient individuals likely to move to areas where there higher skilled jobs (e.g. Antwerp and Brussels – of which Flemish Brabant is the periphery). Understanding these regional differences in skills is important as individuals with lower levels of literacy are more likely to have poorer labour market outcomes relative to those with higher skills.

Mapping the institutional framework for employment and skills policies

Belgium is a federal state, where competences are divided among the federal (national) level, the regions (which encompass the territorial divisions of Flanders, Wallonia and Brussels) and the communities (a division organised by language: Dutch, French or German speaking). There are also provinces, cities, and municipalities which mainly implement federal and regional decisions.

Figure 1.5. **OECD Survey of Adult Skills, results across regions in Flanders**

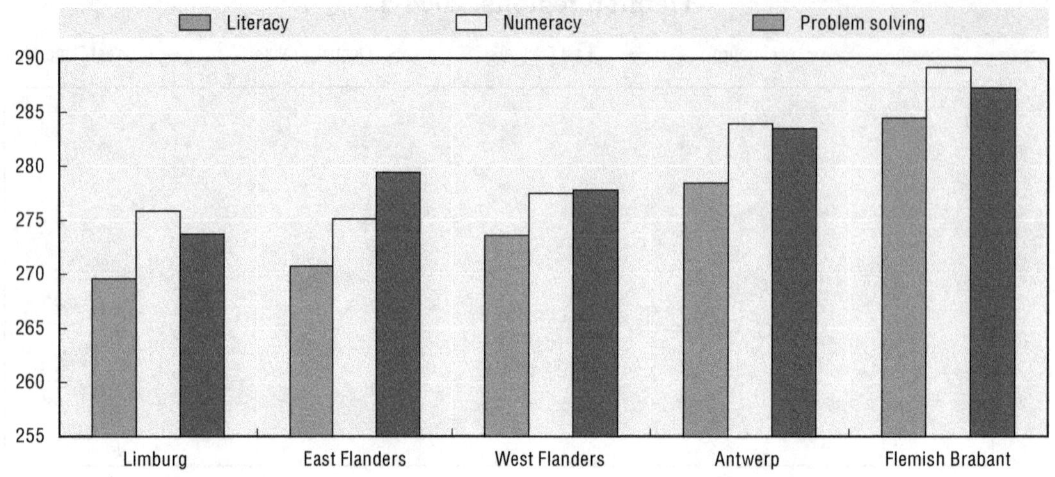

Source: OECD (2013c), *OECD Survey of Adult Skills*.

All levels can take actions related to labour market policy. These powers are mutually exclusive: a power exercised by the federal level cannot be exercised by another level and vice versa. This division of powers and more specifically the transfer of powers to the regions started in the late 1970s and the process of state reform is still ongoing, as the sixth state reform is in the final stage. The federal state is responsible for labour law and social security (e.g. legislation/financing/administration of unemployment, pensions, health and disability insurance).

The regions are responsible for the so-called "territorial matters" (matters related to the region in a broad sense). Economic and employment policies are considered to be territorial matters so the regions have powers related to active labour market policies, labour mediation, and the social economy. The powers associated with the communities are related to the individual. The communities deal with matters such as education and training, assistance to individuals (e.g. support for handicapped persons and immigrant assistance). These responsibilities also include vocational education and training, adult education, literacy programmes, language training and civic integration policies.

Provinces are responsible for everything in their territory residual to the interests of the federal state, the regions and communities. Cities and municipalities can cover everything that is in the interest of the collective needs of their inhabitants. They mainly implement decisions taken at the higher levels, and can develop initiatives of local importance, also related to local labour market policy, education and social welfare. However, local authorities do not receive specific funding for labour market initiatives (except for the so-called central cities who do receive contributions to support their co-ordination role in relation to the local services economy – see below – and who can use the "City Fund" to finance additional costs of regional co-ordination). Cities and municipalities usually have an alderman who is responsible for the local economy, and some also have a local employment department. Local authorities are legally allowed to operate as director with regard to local labour market policy. This role has to be defined in partnership agreements. Flanders consists of five provinces and 308 cities and municipalities. Due to the division of powers articulated above, regional governments each develop different policies and administrative practices.

Active labour market policies in Flanders

Flemish labour market policy is developed using both regional and community competences. Many topics are covered, including diversity in the workplace, entrepreneurship, public and private labour mediation, social economy, employment measures, labour migration, sectoral policies and active restructuring. Flemish educational policy covers aspects related to labour market policy, such as career guidance, collaboration between the educational system and the labour market. As in other countries, policy is developed according to the European frameworks and strategies.

The division of competences creates a system where different actors and institutions are involved in the field of employment policy, operating at various policy levels. Policy instruments and activities take many forms, and are made and delivered not only by the institutions, but also by platforms, partnerships, counsels and co-operation mechanisms.

The management of employment services

The majority of labour market policies in Belgium are managed at the regional level by four public employment services, which cover the Belgian territory. Within Flanders, VDAB (the Flemish public employment service) offers employment services, career services, vocational training and assessment of competences, and manages the majority of Flemish labour market activation measures.

Services are offered to both the unemployed and employed. With regard to the unemployed, VDAB is responsible for registration and placement. Part of the services offered are preventive, part are curative. Comprehensiveness is an important feature of the VDAB approach. The guidance model used consists of different stages, with several modules, to provide services tailored to the needs of jobseekers and the long term unemployed.

VDAB also performs the role of director of labour market and facilitates the functioning of the local labour market. This means that VDAB has to stimulate collaboration with other actors and create partnerships to align services with other labour market actors. The role of director also includes making strategic choices, based on information and expected evolutions in the labour market.

Recently, VDAB has been reorganised to provide more flexibility in the management of employment policies to the local level. There is a central steering organisation and several central support services, but there is also an intermediate provincial structure being given autonomy, on top of 13 regional labour market offices. The local offices can implement and use the centrally provided measures with a certain degree of autonomy. A small proportion of their budgets can be used flexibly to support local projects covering specific local needs.

Other actors involved with employment and skills policies at the local level

At the local level, a number of different actors and stakeholders are involved in the design and implementation of employment and skills policies:

Public Social Welfare Centre (OCMW)

The OCMW is a local government agency which provides social assistance to individuals including income support and guidance to those with insufficient or no social security rights (roughly 1% of the Flemish population). Limited services are also available to asylum seekers and people without legal residence. These centres also play a role in labour market policy through social inclusion and support employment for those confronted with severe difficulties with regard to labour market participation. These centres develop their own activation, training and employment policies and initiatives. This is easier for large centres with larger budgets (means are provided by the cities or municipalities) or those who have partnerships established than for small individual operating centres. Some larger OCMWs have their own employment agency, while smaller OCMWs have to cluster in order to organise such an agency.

Local Employment Agencies (PWA)

Local employment agencies (*Plaatselijk Werkgelegenheidsagentschap* – PWA) are agencies established by (or groups of) communities in order to assist the long-term unemployed, older unemployed, and people on social assistance. These people are employed by the PWA in jobs which include small repair or maintenance work, household assistance, and other occasional administrative tasks. Individuals, local authorities, not for profit organisations, and schools can make use of the services of the people employed by the PWA for a reduced fee. The PWAs are non-profit organisations and are embedded in one-stop job shops (*werkwinkels*).

Local Services Economy

The local services economy (*lokale diensteneconomie*) provides jobs for people who do not manage to find and keep a job in the regular economy. The services delivered by the local services economy are also additional to services delivered in the regular economy such as home care, child care, doing groceries, and maintenance of bicycle tracks. The aim is to create sustainable employment for groups at risk, providing intensive guidance. The supply of these services is co-ordinated by the local authorities. They have to decide upon the services to be delivered taking into account the local needs for services and employment for groups at risk.

The importance of collective bargaining and social dialogue in Flanders

In Flanders, there is a strong network of councils and committees which influence skills policies involving social partners including trade unions (representing the employed as well as the unemployed) and employer's organisations. Collective bargaining with regard to advice and decision-making is very important in the field of socio-economic policy making and implementation. An important feature is "parity" where both parties are considered to be equal.

At the Flemish level, the SERV and VESOC play a role in fostering social dialogue. The SERV (Flemish Socio-Economical Council – *Sociaal-Economische Raad van Vlaanderen*) is a consultative body of employer's organisations and the trade unions. The SERV is an advisory body for the Flemish government related to socio-economic topics. It focuses on issues such as work and the social economy, education and training, social protection, diversity and innovation. The VESOC (Flemish Economic Social Consultation Committee – *Vlaams Economisch Sociaal Overlegcomité*) is a consultative body, where employer's organisations and trade unions debate with the Flemish government on social and economic topics. If consensus is reached, the Flemish government is obliged to act according to the consensus.

At the sub-regional level, the SERR and RESOC are subsidised by the Flemish government and have a strategic role in formulating labour market policies and programmes. Their influence on programmes and policies depends on local institutional and political circumstances. Many other organisations such as the public employment services and the

National Employment Service include representatives of the social partners on their boards or management committees.

The SERR (Socio-Economic Council of the Region – *Sociaal-economische raad van de regio*) gives advice to the different governments and local authorities with regard to economic and labour market policy. These councils are obliged to give advice when asked for, but they can also give advice on their own initiative. They are expected to formulate specific advice on the yearly action plans of VDAB, its local project programme, vocational training programmes and diversity plans. This council also organises consultations regarding socio-economic matters of importance to the region. There are 16 representatives, which include employers (including SMEs), as well as trade unions which are appointed by the SERV. This council supports enterprises with the diversification of their workforce, by developing Diversity Plans (*diversiteitsplannen*). There are 13 SERRs in Flanders and their staffing and operations are supported by the Flemish government. Additional financing can be provided by the provinces or through European projects.

The RESOC (Regional Economic and Social Consultation Committee – *Regionaal Economisch en Sociaal Overlegcomité*) gives advice to cities and communities, the province, the Flemish and also the federal government about socio-economic matters. Advice has to be given with regard to start-up centres for the social economy, insertion companies, sheltered workplaces, the local job shops, work experience projects, and the local services economy. This committee is also responsible for drafting the "pact of the region" (*streekpact*). This document includes the opinion of local authorities and the social partners on the development of the region for a six year period. The RESOC deals with issues such as skills shortages and hard-to-fill vacancies, the alignment of education and the labour market, and the mobility of workers. Advice from the RESOC is expected to be based on a thorough analysis of the local labour market situation. A RESOC consists of the 16 members of the SERR, and at least 8 representatives of the province, the cities and municipalities. There are 15 RESOCs operating in Flanders and similar to SERRs, funding is provided by the Flemish government, the provinces (and the Provincial Development Agency) and European subsidies (ESF/ERDF).

Vocational education and training system (VET)

In Flanders, education is compulsory until the age of 18 (full-time until the age of 16). Secondary education includes three stages (two years each). After a comprehensive first stage, the second stage offers vocational options, to be completed in the third stage. The full-time track offers general education (ASO), technical education (TSO) and vocational education (BSO). The part-time track is offered by vocational secondary schools (one or two days at school and three or four days of other activities, such as labour participation (paid or unpaid work, volunteering), preparatory trajectories and bridging projects for those not having the basic skills or attitudes) or personal development trajectories (intensive individual guidance for severely disadvantaged pupils).

After secondary education, many VET programmes are available in the educational system: "secondary-after-secondary" in secondary schools (Se-n-Se), associate degree programmes offered by adult education centres and university colleges, and professional bachelor programmes provided by university colleges.

Adult education centres provide skills development activities in 420 different programmes at the secondary level and the number of students enrolled has increased significantly in recent years. In 2007, programmes have been modular and can be combined with general education to lead to a diploma of secondary education (Musset, 2013). Programmes provided in secondary schools, centres for adult education, and university colleges are supervised by the Flemish Department of Education with the exception of a few vocational programmes which are under the responsibility of other ministries of the Flemish community (Musset, 2013).

Vocational training is also provided by the Flemish public employment service (VDAB), which is an autonomous agency that reports to the Minister of Work and Social Economy. Complete programmes geared towards specific occupations are offered, but also courses which develop key competences or specific technical skills, tailored to the needs of the local labour market. Vocational training and the assessment of competences is organised and managed by 87 competence centres (*competentiecentra*) grouped in 40 campuses.

Many sectoral training funds offer training for the employed or for job-seekers aiming to work in a specific sector. These funds provide training and different types of support to employers and other training institutions. The provision of training and assistance is often supported through sectoral covenants, which are agreements between the social partners within specific economic sectors and the Flemish government. Sectoral training funds often collaborate with secondary schools or post-secondary education providers, in order to enhance the quality of training provided.

Syntra Flanders – Flemish Agency for Entrepreneurship

Syntra Flanders, the Flemish Agency for Entrepreneurship (*Vlaams Agentschap voor Ondernemersvorming*) is responsible for the promotion of entrepreneurship and a provider of vocational training. It operates under the supervision of the Department of Work and Social Economy with ties also to the Department of Education. It subsidies and monitors 24 training centres across Flanders, providing 500 different vocational programmes within 28 sectors.

Syntra also has a mandate to promote entrepreneurship, the development of entrepreneurial skills within the education and training system, and to provide flexible and co-ordinated training services. Syntra offers apprenticeship training enabling individuals to spend one day per week in a training centre and four days a week in a company learning on the job. Their courses are open to the general public but aim more specifically at preparing self-employed entrepreneurs, giving them the technical and managerial skills to start and operate their own company.

Regional technological centres (RTC)

Regional technological centres are collaborative partnerships between the educational system and enterprises. They do not provide VET, but they facilitate connections between companies and secondary schools or adult education centres, in order to create workplace training opportunities, the sharing of equipment and infrastructure, and training of teachers. There are 5 RTC's, which operate at the level of provinces and stimulate the exchange of good practices. They are accountable to the Flemish government and have to develop strategic plans every five years, and yearly action plans.

The role of social partners in education and training

The government is advised by the social partners (trade unions and employer organisations) through the Flemish Education Council (*Vlaamse Onderwijsraad* – VLOR). This council also includes the educational umbrella organisations, centres for pupil guidance, teachers, parents, students and principals. As mentioned before, the SERV is engaged with the Flemish VET system and provides advice with regard to education and training, especially when it comes to vocational education and training and the relationship between education and the labour market.

References

Bulté, Steven and Ludo Struyven (2013), *The Belgian labour market after 5 years of crisis: Never before has the degree of job creation been so low*, DynaM Analysis, December 2013

Bogaerts, K. et al. (2011), "Building Flexibility and Accountability Into Local Employment Services: Country Report for Belgium", *OECD Local Economic and Employment Development (LEED) Working Papers*, No. 2011/11, OECD Publishing, Paris, *http://dx.doi.org/10.1787/5kg3mkv0448s-en*.

Flemish Department of Education and Training (2013), "Vocational Education and Training in Flanders", *Country Background Report*, OECD review of Postsecondary Vocational Education and Training.

OECD (2014a), *OECD Regional Outlook 2014: Regions and Cities: Where Policies and People Meet*, OECD Publishing, Paris, *http://dx.doi.org/10.1787/9789264201415-en*.

OECD (2014b), *OECD Employment Outlook 2014*, OECD Publishing, Paris, *http://dx.doi.org/10.1787/empl_outlook-2014-en*.

OECD (2013a), *OECD Economic Surveys: Belgium 2013*, OECD Publishing, Paris, *doi: http://dx.doi.org/10.1787/eco_surveys-bel-2013-en*.

OECD (2013b), *Education at a Glance 2013: OECD Indicators*, OECD Publishing, Paris, *http://dx.doi.org/10.1787/eag-2013-en*.

OECD (2013c), *OECD Skills Outlook 2013: First Results from the Survey of Adult Skills*, OECD Publishing, Paris, *http://dx.doi.org/10.1787/9789264204256-en*.

Musset, P (2013), *A Skills Beyond School Commentary on Flanders*, OECD Publishing, *www.oecd.org/edu/skills-beyond-school/ASkillsBeyondSchoolCommentaryOnFlanders.pdf*.

Zimmer, H. (2012), "Labour market mismatches", *Economic Review*, National Bank of Belgium, September.

Chapter 2

Overview of the Flanders, Belgium case study areas

To better understand the role of the local level in contributing to job creation and productivity, this review examined local activities in two Flemish regions: Antwerp; and Limburg. This chapter provides a labour market and economic overview of each region as well as the results from an OECD LEED statistical tool which looks at the relationship between skills supply and demand at the sub-national level.

Overview of the case study areas

Flanders is one of the three regions in Belgium, having 6 280 000 inhabitants. Over 10 years, the population increased by 6% with about 65% of the inhabitants aged between 15-64 years old. The Flemish labour market is not homogeneous, with many sub-regional and local differences. The cities in particular are confronted with persistent high levels of unemployment.

City of Antwerp

Antwerp is the largest city in Flanders (more than 500 000 inhabitants), situated in the province of Antwerp. It is located a mere 40 km north of Brussels, the capital of Belgium. The city has an extensive road network, a high-speed train station and a business airport. The port of Antwerp, the second largest in Europe, is located inland and connected with the North Sea. Antwerp is affected by many demographic and labour market developments, such as increased migration, high youth unemployment, and rising long-term unemployment.

Figure 2.1. **Map of Antwerp**

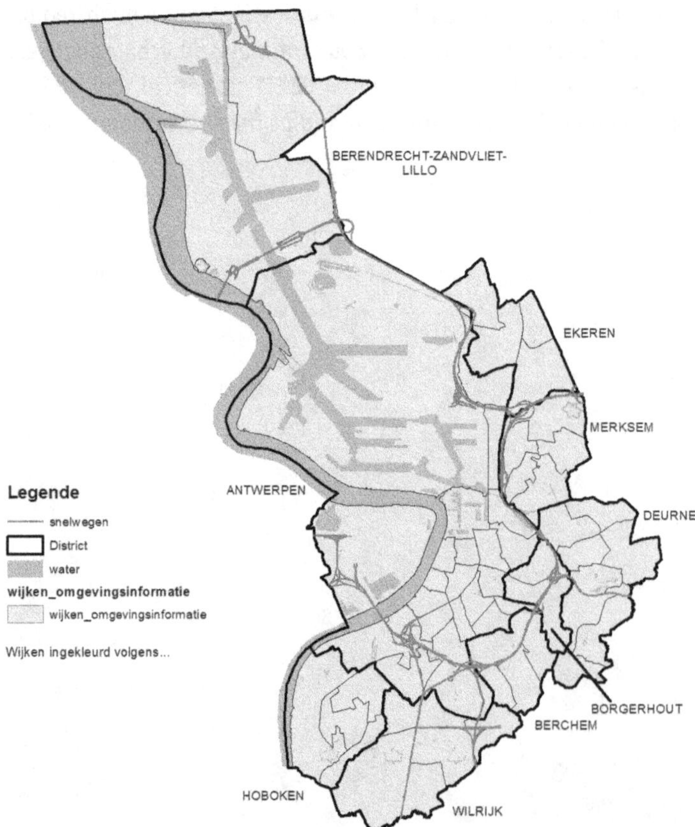

Source: Stad Antwerpen – studiedienst stadsobservatie GIS (*City of Antwerp engineering department observation*).

Limburg

Limburg is one of five Flemish provinces, situated in the east, adjoining the Netherlands and located close to Germany. The area is 2 414 km^2. West of the province, it borders the provinces of Antwerp and Flemish-Brabant (enclosing the capital of Belgium, Brussels). South of the province lies the Walloon province Liège. The province is strongly influenced by its past as a mining region, having attracted many migrants mainly in the 1950s and 1960s. After the closure of the mines, mainly in the 1980s, the province went through a process of conversion.

Figure 2.2. **Map of the Limburg region**

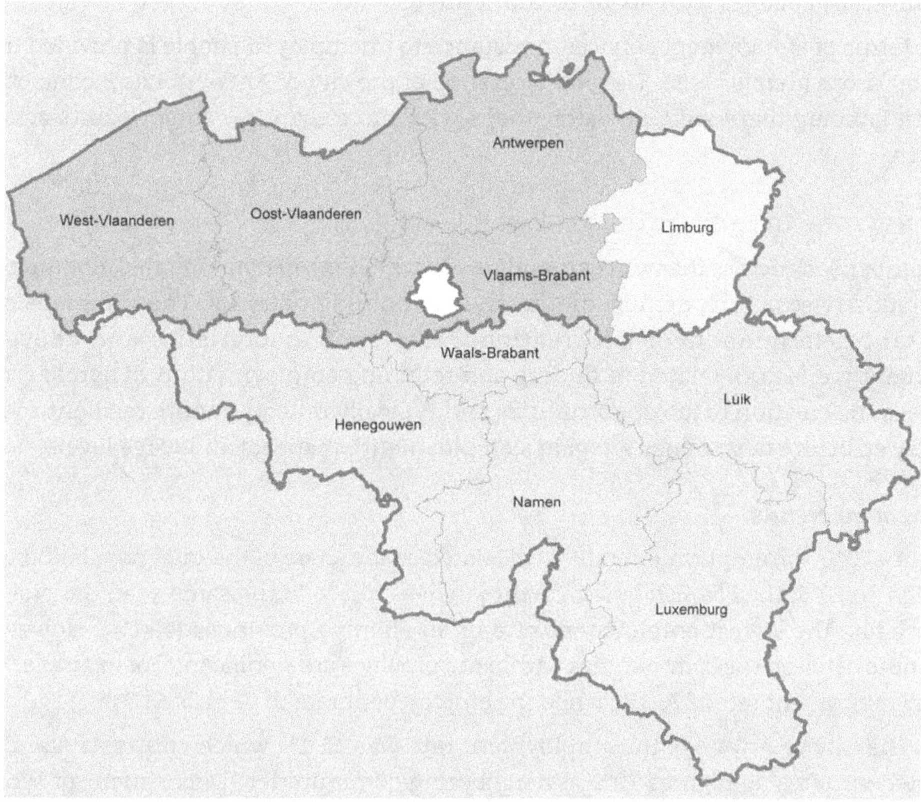

Source: *GIS Limburg* – Provincie Limburg (*Province of Limburg*).

The province has been seriously impacted by the crisis and by the announcement of the closure of the plant of Ford Genk where it is estimated that 8 000 jobs will be destroyed. This will in turn have significant impacts on employment, directly and indirectly through the impact on supply companies in the region. One of the aims of the conversion of the province is to make Limburg less dependent on a limited number of industries, and to develop new sectors, such as clean-tech, logistics and the care sector. Public transport is less developed in this region than in other parts of Flanders, and many businesses cannot be reached easily by the road or railway network.

Provision of education and presence of employment services

Vocational education and training is well developed in Flanders. However, in secondary education students (or their parents) tend to favour the general track over the technical and vocational tracks, leading often to hard-to-fill vacancies with regard to technical and vocational professions. Antwerp has several adult education centres within the city while Limburg has 20 centres across the province. The public employment service (VDAB) has its own training centres (called competence centres), which are organised provincially and have several local establishments, including three in Antwerp and 13 across the province of Limburg.

Antwerp has one university with more than 12 000 students enrolled in 2012-13 and three university colleges with 28 000 students. Several knowledge centres are linked to the university or the colleges in the fields of management, sustainable development, logistics, and medicine. Limburg has one university with more than 9 000 students in 2011-12 and four university colleges with about 16 000 students.

In terms of employment services, assistance to unemployed people is provided through one-stop shops (*werkwinkels*). The one-stop shop of the city of Antwerp has 8 contact points while in Limburg there are 5 one-stop shops with more than 30 contact points across the province.

Comparison across the case study areas

Comparisons across the two case study areas include employment rates, unemployment rates, industry structure, demographics, and commuting patterns. These dimensions are important determinants of job creation. Personal characteristics and educational attainment are factors related to finding and retaining employment. A dynamic economy increases the creation of job opportunities and typically reflects a more resilient economy. Industry structure determines a region's employment prospects and wage levels.

Employment trends

Since 2010, the employment rate is calculated as the share of the total population of 20-64 year olds. In 2012, the Flemish employment rate was 71.5%. In the same year, the province of Limburg had the lowest employment rate of all Flemish provinces (69.2%). However, the differences between the communities within the province are significant. For example, Hasselt has an employment rate of 70.1%, while the employment rate of Genk is 61.2%.

In the City of Antwerp, the employment rate was 62.1% which contrasts starkly with employment rates as high as 70% in neighboring communities (Department of Work and Social Economy, 2013). The employment rate is lower for women compared to men, especially in regions with low employment rates. Furthermore, older workers and the disabled tend to have lower employment rates than the average.

Residents of the study areas vary in diversity and in educational attainment. Both the region of Limburg and the City of Antwerp have a highly trained workforce. In the province of Antwerp, 35% of the persons aged 25-64 have graduated from tertiary education. Typical for the Flemish labour force is the command of languages. Dutch is the native language, but most people also speak at least another language, such as English and French. Many also have a command of German, Spanish or other languages.

Unemployment

The unemployment rate is the share of unemployed jobseekers in the labour force between 15-64 years old. In 2012, unemployment in Flanders was 6.9%, which represents an increase of 25.2% compared to 2008. The province of Limburg has the highest unemployment rate of all Flemish provinces (7.4%), which will increase further following the closure of the Ford factory. Antwerp demonstrates how unemployment can be concentrated in bigger cities in Flanders. In 2012, unemployment was 14.9%, which was one of the highest rates in Flanders.

Low skilled persons are over-represented in the group of unemployed jobseekers. Of all unemployed jobseekers, half are low skilled. Older workers (over 50), migrants, and disabled persons also represent a significant share of the unemployed. In Limburg, unemployment rates are especially high among youth and women.

Industry structure

In both Antwerp and Limburg, employment is concentrated mainly in two economic activities, namely public administration, defence, education, health care, and social work; and wholesale retail trade, transport, accommodation, and food services (see Table 2.1). In 2012, the former represented 28.7% of employment in the City of Antwerp and 32.7% in the region of Limburg and the latter was 25.7% in the City of Antwerp and 23.1% in the region of Limburg. Another important sector is industry, which represented 17.4% of employment in the Limburg region and 17% in the City of Antwerp.

Table 2.1. **Employment by economic activity, 2012**

%

	Belgium	Antwerp	Limburg
Agriculture, forestry and fishing	1.2	0.7	0.9
Industry (except construction)	14.6	17.0	17.4
Construction	7.2	6.7	7.7
Wholesale retail trade, transport, accommodation, food service	22.5	25.7	23.1
Information and communications	3.3	3.4	2.2
Financial and insurance	3.5	3.7	2.4
Real estate	0.6	0.4	0.4
Professional, scientific, technical, administrative, support service	9.9	10.1	9.4
Public administration, defence, education, human health, social work	32.6	28.7	32.7
Arts, entertainment, recreation	4.8	3.4	3.8

Demographics

In 2012, the city of Antwerp had 502 604 inhabitants. In 10 years, the population has increased by 12%. The province of Limburg has 849 404 inhabitants (a 6 % increase in 10 years) (ADSEI, 2012). It is clear that Flanders is confronted with an ageing population. In 2000, there were 112 persons between 15-25 years old for every 100 persons aged 55-64 years. It is expected that this ratio will decrease and will be 78 in 2020.

Commuting patterns

A recent study of labour force mobility shows that Flanders contains 14 local labour markets which are areas where people live as well as work, or where they work in a limited number of identifiable communities (Vanderbiesen, Herremans & Sels, 2013). Antwerp forms a local labour market together with the city of Sint-Niklaas and surrounding communities totalling 51 communalities and more than 500 000 employed persons. This is quite exceptional as most local labour markets do not cross provincial borders, and Sint-Niklaas is situated in the province of East-Flanders.

This local labour market has an employment self-containment ratio of 75%. This means that 75% of the employed persons in this region live and work there. In the province of Limburg, three local labour markets can be distinguished: the region adjoining the Netherlands (ratio: 56.7%), Hasselt-Sint-Truiden (ratio: 54.3%) and Genk (ratio: 50.2%). With regard to Genk, 16% of the employed work in Hasselt, the others work mainly in other Limburg communalities. It is questioned whether the area of Genk will remain a so-called local labour market after the closure of the Ford plant. This will depend on the success of the conversion and job creation measures. However, considering the province as a whole, more inhabitants work outside the province (e.g. in the province of Antwerp or in the province of Flemish-Brabant (Brussels and Leuven, or even the Netherlands) (VDAB, 2013).

Balance between skills supply and demand at the sub-national level

The LEED Programme has developed a statistical tool to understand the balance between skills supply and demand within local labour markets (Froy, Giguère and Meghnagi, 2012). In the Flemish context, this tool can help to provide policy makers with an understanding of skills mismatches, which may occur at the sub-national level. It can inform place-based policy approaches at the local level.

Figure 2.3. **Understanding the relationship between skills supply and demand**

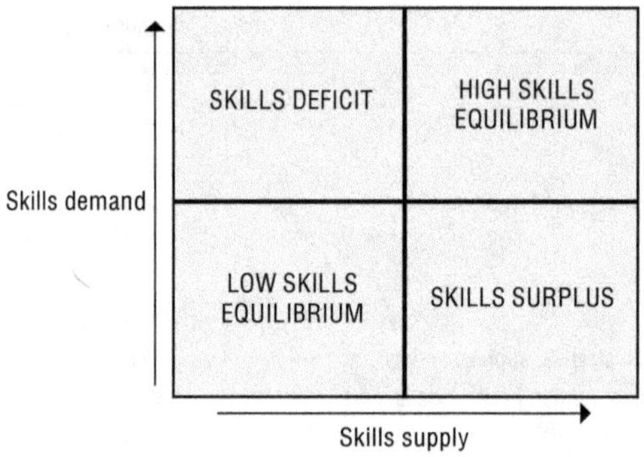

Source: Froy, F. and S. Giguère (2010), "Putting in Place Jobs that Last: A Guide to Rebuilding Quality Employment at Local Level", *OECD Local Economic and Employment Development (LEED) Working Papers*, No. 2010/13, OECD Publishing, *http://dx.doi.org/10.1787/5km7jf7qtk9p-en.*

Looking at the figure above, in the top-left corner (skills gaps and shortages), demand for high skills is met by a supply of low skills, a situation that results in reported skills gaps and shortages. In the top-right corner, demand for high skills is met by an equal supply of high skills resulting in a high-skill equilibrium. This is the most desired destination of all high performing local economies. At the bottom-left corner the demand for low skills is met by a supply of low skills resulting in a low-skill equilibrium. The challenge facing policymakers is to get the economy moving in a north-easterly direction towards the top-right corner. Lastly, in the bottom-right corner, demand for low skills is met by a supply of high skills resulting in an economy where what high skills are available are not utilised. This leads to the out migration of talent, underemployment, skill under-utilisation, and attrition of human capital, all of which signal missed opportunities for creating prosperity.

This typology was applied to Belgium and the region of Flanders, including the case study regions of Antwerp and Limburg – see Figures 2.4-2.6 below. The analysis positions regions relative to each other and does not compare with other regions within the OECD.

Box 2.1. **Explaining the diagnostic tool**

The analysis is carried out at Territorial Level 3 regions (regions with populations ranging between 150 000-800 000). The supply of skills was measured by the percentage of the population with post-secondary education. The demand for skills was measured by the percentage of the population employed in medium-high skilled occupations. Regions are also classified in relation to the average state unemployment rate. The indices are standardised using the inter-decile method and are compared with the national median. Further explanations on the methodology can be found in Froy, Giguère and Meghnagi, 2012.

Source: Froy, F., S. Giguère and M. Meghnagi (2012), "Skills for Competitiveness: A Synthesis Report", *OECD Local Economic and Employment Development (LEED) Working Papers*, No. 2012/09, OECD Publishing, *http://dx.doi.org/10.1787/5k98xwskmvr6-en.*

Figure 2.4. **Skills supply and demand in Belgium, TL2 regions, 2010**

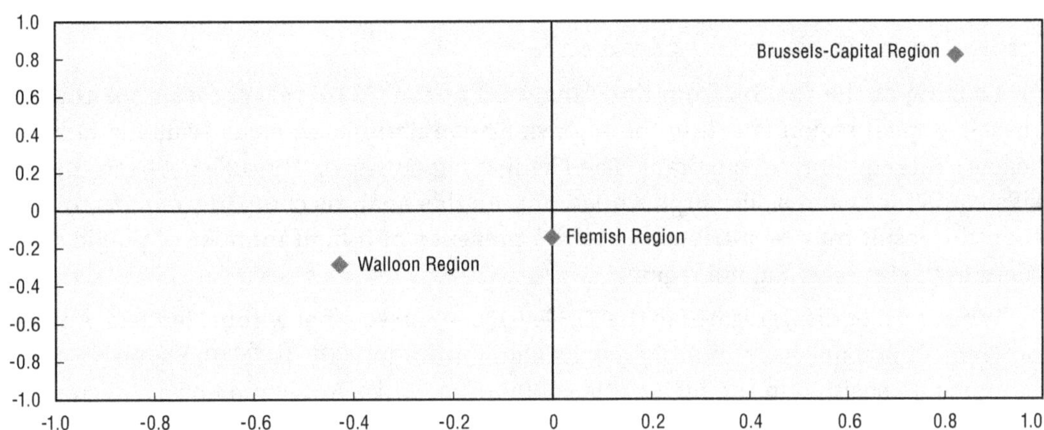

Source: Author's calculations based on Labour Force Survey, Statistics Belgium and Bank of Belgium.

Figure 2.5. **Skills supply and demand in Belgium, TL3 regions, 2001**

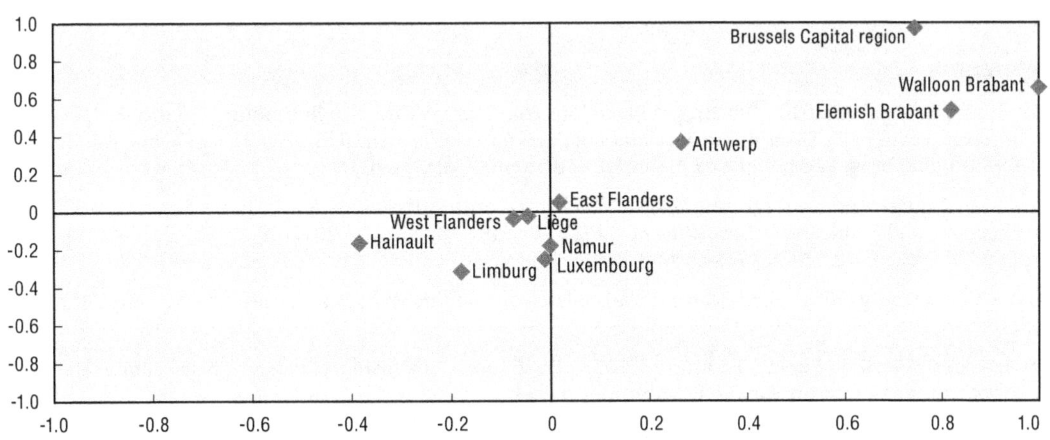

Source: Author's calculations Labour Force Survey, Statistics Belgium and Bank of Belgium.

Figure 2.6. **Skills supply and demand in Belgium, TL3 regions, 2010**

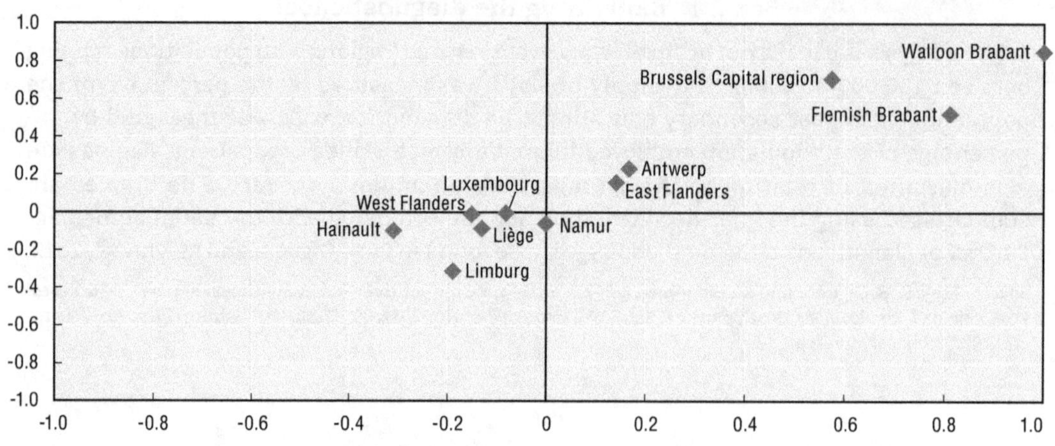

Source: Author's calculations Labour Force Survey, Statistics Belgium and Bank of Belgium.

Results from the data mapping exercise

Looking at the results from data analysed at the TL2 level, one can see that the Brussels-Capital region falls into the high-skills equilibrium, whereas Wallonia falls into the low skills equilibrium quadrant. The Flemish region sits on the axis between the low-skills equilibrium and skills surplus quadrant. As this analysis compares regions to each-other, the result may be attributable to the presence of a high number of public sector offices in the Brussels-Capital region.

When further disaggregated to the TL3 level, one can see that within Flanders, Antwerp and Flemish Brabant were in a high-skills equilibrium in 2001. In 2010, Flemish Brabant maintains its position in the high-skills equilibrium, while Antwerp shows a decrease in both skills supply and demand which suggests a relative loss of competitiveness in the province. In both 2001 and 2010, Limburg falls into the low-skills equilibrium, which means relatively low levels of both skills supply and demand relative to other regions in the province.

References

Froy, F. and S. Giguère (2010), "Putting in Place Jobs that Last: A Guide to Rebuilding Quality Employment at Local Level", *OECD Local Economic and Employment Development (LEED) Working Papers*, No. 2010/13, OECD Publishing, Paris, *http://dx.doi.org/10.1787/5km7jf7qtk9p-en.*

Froy, F., S. Giguère and M. Meghnagi (2012), "Skills for Competitiveness: A Synthesis Report", *OECD Local Economic and Employment Development (LEED) Working Papers*, No. 2012/09, OECD Publishing, Paris, *http://dx.doi.org/10.1787/5k98xwskmvr6-en.*

POM-ERSV Limburg (2014), *Socio-economische analyse van Limburg en haar vijf streken*, POM – ERSV Limburg, Limburg.

Departement Werk en Sociale Economie (2013), *De Vlaamse arbeidsmarkt in kaart. Beleidsbarometer 2012*, Departement Werk en Sociale Economie, Brussel.

Vanderbiesen, W. et al. (2013), *Afbakening en profiel van lokale arbeidsmarkten in Vlaanderen* (WSE Report 6-2013), Steunpunt Werk en Sociale Economie, Leuven.

VDAB (2013), *Provincie Limburg & de Limburgse streektafels. Een socio-economische analyse*, VDAB, Brussel.

Chapter 3

Local Job Creation Dashboard findings in Flanders, Belgium

This chapter highlights findings from the Local Job Creation Dashboard in Flanders. The findings are discussed through the four thematic areas of the OECD review: 1) better aligning policies and programmes to local employment development; 2) adding value through skills; 3) targeting policy to local employment sectors and investing in quality jobs; and 4) being inclusive.

Results from the dashboard

This section of the report presents the key findings from the in-depth fieldwork undertaken in Flanders. In this chapter, each of the four priority areas of the OECD review on local job creation policies are discussed sequentially, accompanied by an explanation of the results.

The full results of the Local Job Creation Dashboard across Flanders are presented in Figure 3.1 below. The dashboard enables national and local policy makers to gain a stronger overview of the strengths and weaknesses in the implementation of employment and skills policies, while better prioritising future actions. The values in the dashboard were obtained through a standard OECD methodology which collects a range of quantitative and qualitative information and assigns a value between 1 (low) and 5 (high) based on LEED research and best practices in other OECD countries. The same methodology has been applied to all OECD countries participating in the OECD reviews on local job creation.

Figure 3.1. **Local Job Creation Dashboard – Flanders**

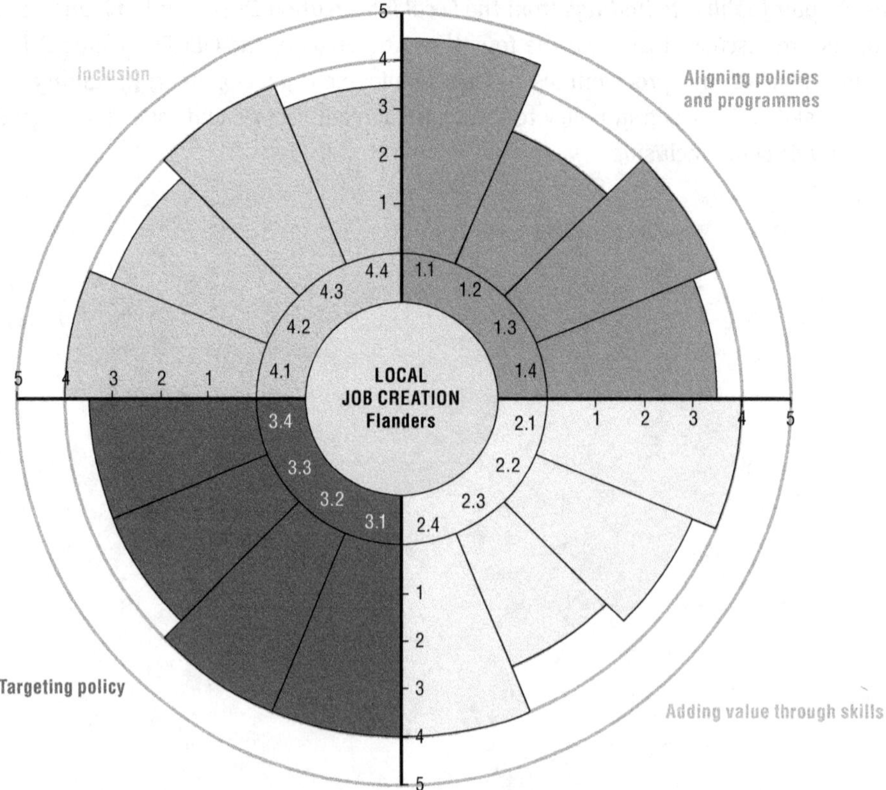

Theme 1: Better aligning policy and programmes to local economic development

Flexibility in the delivery of employment and vocational training policies

The OECD defines flexibility as "the possibility to adjust policy at its various design, implementation and delivery stages to make it better adapted to local contexts, actions carried out by other organisations, strategies being pursued, and challenges and opportunities faced" (Froy and Giguère, 2009). Flexibility deals with the latitude that exists in the management of the employment and training system, rather than the flexibility in the labour market itself. The achievement of local flexibility does not necessarily mean that governments need to politically decentralise (Froy and Giguère, 2009). Governments just need to give sufficient latitude when allocating responsibilities in the fields of designing policies and programmes, managing budgets, setting performance targets, deciding on eligibility and outsourcing services.

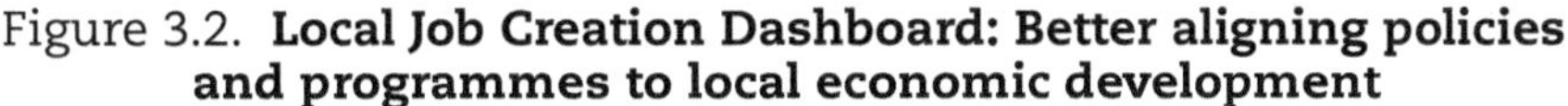

Figure 3.2. **Local Job Creation Dashboard: Better aligning policies and programmes to local economic development**

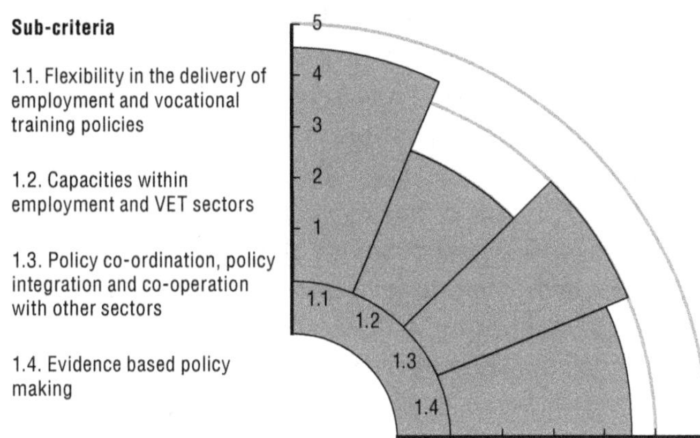

A previous study was conducted in Flanders by the OECD on the accountability and flexibility within the employment system (see Bogaerts et al., 2011). With regard to local employment agencies, the study found that there was still room for further flexibility at the local level with the possibility for local projects and other local initiatives to be strengthened and for collaboration to be organised more strategically. The study noted that collaboration at many different governance levels had been supported, but it made the labour market policy planning process very complicated.

Finally, this previous OECD review concluded that the capacities at the local level could be raised but that this required local employment offices to gain sufficient responsibility as well as a degree of control over policy implementation. Since this study, several changes have been made by VDAB to make the employment services more flexible, enabling local offices to take a more strategic leadership role in designing and implementing policies.

Flexibility within employment services offered by VDAB

VDAB has an agreement (*beheersovereenkomst*) with the Flemish Government that defines 5 strategic objectives: 1) to activate all job seekers and other non-active citizens by using an individual approach, aiming at sustainable integration into the labour market; 2) to provide career guidance for every working citizen; 3) to support employers to hire well qualified employees; 4) to provide procedures that recognise and develop competences; and 5) to create partnerships.

Flexibility in the delivery of services is a key feature of the organisational structure of VDAB. Recently, more autonomy has been given to the provincial level. Local employment service offices are directed by provincial management in order to be more flexible and targeted to the local labour market. The provincial board of directors (*provinciaal directie comité*) takes decisions autonomously by developing a provincial plan within the overall framework of the Flemish business plan which contains a number of strategic objectives. Within each province, local employment offices also have a certain degree of autonomy through flexible budgets (e.g. 15% of the budget line), which enable them to develop programmes and policies in partnership with other stakeholders. During interviews undertaken for this study, it was acknowledged that the flexibility of public employment services will be even more necessary in the future to ensure employment programmes and policies can be adjusted to local labour market conditions.

Performance management within employment programmes

Performance agreements between VDAB and the Flemish government contain strategic and operational objectives. For each objective, indicators are chosen and monitored to manage performance. If possible, a target is chosen that might be adjusted over the years - when progression is made and the target is reached, a new target is chosen. These targets are part of the provincial business plans that are formulated annually. Both business plans use input from sectoral business plans. Local employment offices are free to choose targets for their own local projects that have been launched with the flexible funding available to them. Monitoring is done at different levels: the Flemish level, the provincial level, and the regional level. Performance objectives include

- Inputs and procedures: number of people reached by the competence centres, number of contracts signed for Individual Vocational Training, and the number of guidance processes (preventive or remedial) started for job seekers.
- Satisfaction: satisfaction of job seekers, clients of the one-stop shops, as well as employers.
- Socio-economic outcomes, such as transition to employment after the guidance process.

All general information about VDAB and employment services is publicly available but performance management reports concerning individual local employment offices are not shared publicly. However, as there are several agreements with local partners, local offices have to report about activities and results to these stakeholders involved. The local employment offices of VDAB also have to report about performance to the regional consultation bodies.

Outsourcing arrangements

VDAB often makes use of the services of commercial and non-commercial organisations with regard to guidance and training. Tenders are published by the central services of VDAB, but regional tenders are also common. The conditions in these regional tenders are usually strict. The provincial board of directors decides whether services should be outsourced or not and to whom based on the outcome of the tendering process. Outsourcing officers are appointed and during the last few years, the budget for outsourcing has been steadily increased.

Flexibility in local training provision

There is a high level of flexibility within the vocational education and training system in Flanders as a result of the autonomy granted to individual organisations. With regard to training programmes, the Flemish government defines goals or basic competences to be reached, which are derived from recognised frameworks (e.g. a vocational profile recognised by the Flemish government or by sectoral bodies). Training providers have to develop their programmes in line with these competences however, they can decide which pedagogical approaches or didactical methods will be used. New training programmes have to be approved by the Flemish government. A procedure for approvals has been established and the Flemish Educational Council (VLOR) gives advice to the Flemish government about new programmes.

The training centres of VDAB and Syntra have a high degree of flexibility and can easily respond to the needs of local actors. Local actors are regularly consulted, and requests from local actors for special training programmes are often taken into account. New training programmes can be provided in a timely manner and the curriculum can be designed locally. Both VDAB and Syntra plan provision on the basis of an analysis of the local economic context and rely on consultation with local stakeholders.

Capacities within employment and VET sectors

VDAB's staffing resources are under pressure due to budget cuts by the Flemish government. Since 2012, VDAB has had to cut 325 staff, representing 6.5% of total employees, adding further pressure on existing staff. During the local interviews undertaken for this study, it was highlighted that staffing resources are perceived to be adequate for implementing the current workload although there is a perceived risk of compromising the quality of the services because of the increased tasks being taken on by existing employment services staff.

VDAB has its own training centre where each employee is offered five days of training every year. Team leaders make training plans and conferences are organised where current topics are discussed and presented. During team meetings, employees are invited to participate in discussions. Overall, the skill levels of staff are perceived to be sufficient for implementing the organisational objectives effectively.

In order to support the design of interventions at the local level, the central services of VDAB provide guidance, tools and instruments to local offices. These central services include:

- follow up on European labour market policy events and research reports where information is shared with local stakeholders;
- the implementation of European instruments such as EURES, EUROPASS; promoting the use of effective tools and instruments, such as e-portfolios;
- collecting, processing and distributing labour market information as well as information about services provided by different actors;
- forecasting needs for services (training, support and guidance, and brokering);
- managing relationships with other labour market actors, target groups, and sectors;
- process management about large-scale tendering; and
- capacity building activities around monitoring, evaluation, and quality assurance.

Policy co-ordination, policy integration and co-operation with other sectors

Since the restructuring of VDAB which provided more autonomy to the provinces, collaborative action has increased through local partnership agreements. In general, these agreements state the general aims and most often describe the division of tasks between the partners and where collaboration will be undertaken. An advantage of this type of formal agreement is that they make it possible to react within a short period of time to changes in the local labour market, often using innovative projects or measures.

Within the area of employment policy, local joint strategies are developed in collaboration which often includes an official formal agreement between stakeholders. VDAB has established formal agreements on collaboration with the provinces (see Box 3.1 for an example from Limburg); various cities/municipalities and OCMWs which deliver social welfares services; one-stop shops (*werkwinkels*); and not-for profit organisations or social enterprises.

Box 3.1. **Local collaboration agreement between VDAB and the province of Limburg**

VDAB and the province are important actors with regard to labour market policy. VDAB is "director" of the labour market providing guidance and training, matching job seekers and employers. The province is responsible for sub-regional socio-economic policy anticipating new sectoral developments, developing and promoting the region, as well as stimulating entrepreneurship.

In 2013, a formal agreement was established to develop and implement integrated policies to reduce unemployment in the province of Limburg, to reduce mismatch between supply and demand, to make the labour market more flexible (in line with new economic developments) and to realise the growth potential in the social economy.

Responsibilities are assigned to each partner in accordance with each partner's expertise, tasks are distributed and services are designed to be complementary. Data will be exchanged between organisations and trends will be monitored. Special attention will be paid to trans-boundary collaboration. The province will take action to engage municipalities and social partners, using the RESOC Limburg consultation body.

While many formal agreements have been made, there are also informal networks and exchanges. For example, the City of Antwerp has an informal network recently established to assist high skilled migrants, which includes VDAB, the City of Antwerp, a reception service for newcomers (*onthaalbureau*), and a centre for the integration of cultural minorities. Informal working groups were established and thematic consultations were undertaken to identify issues and potential actions to improve their labour market outcomes.

In terms of joined-up strategies for job creation, a good example of collaboration at the local level is the Strategic Action Plan for Limburg (SALK – *Strategisch Actieplan Limburg in't Kwadraat*) which involves VDAB, provincial and local governments, employers, social economy enterprises, universities and high-tech scientific research institutes, the Provincial Development Agency, and the Flemish government. This plan was created following recent economic setbacks in the region due to the imminent closure of Ford Genk. In July 2013, the Flemish government released the Action Plan for Limburg, which contains actions that will contribute to local job creation as well as innovative and sustainable entrepreneurship. The objective is the long-term recovery of the region through projects at the regional and local level.

The motivation for the plan was the closure of Ford Genk (announced in 2012 and to be executed by the end of 2014). 6 000 jobs will be lost directly through the closure and an additional 4 000 jobs will be indirectly lost. The Flemish government immediately decided to establish a Task Force consisting of the various local partners to prepare for the reconversion of the region. A group of experts mapped the consequences of the closure and presented policy measures to be taken to develop new activities in the region and to create the pre-conditions for recovery.

Several joint projects are being established to develop skills within the region, including skills development activities for job seekers in collaboration with VDAB and the centres for adult education. Special training programmes for groups at risk and people who are temporarily unemployed are being introduced as well as an increase in apprenticeship training (especially in the care sector). Other projects include increased support for entrepreneurship, developing more robust information on job vacancies and career guidance, as well as preparing people for interviews. A number of infrastructure projects will also be launched including the reconversion of the Ford site, the acceleration of public-private partnerships on certain construction projects (e.g. bridges, railways and tram lines, business parks, as well as renovations of social housing projects).

Joined-up delivery of employment services through local one-stop shops (werkwinkels)

Joined up delivery of employment services is facilitated by local one-stop shops (*werkwinkels*). One-stop shops are established to provide integrated and comprehensive services on work and employment, for job seekers as well as employers. They are non-profit organisations that have been developed into a network, which takes into account the nature and qualities of each actor involved, in order to add value to the customers.

Partners involved include VDAB, OCMW (public welfare centres), labour counselling, the local employment agency (PWA), the national service for employment, specialised guidance centres and other local actors, such as the municipality. Each partner provides part of the financial means necessary to run the one-stop shop and to deliver services to job seekers and employers.

These one-stop shops contribute to better labour market performance by enhancing each jobseeker's ability to self-manage his or her career and to provide individual coaching for those who need it. In 2009, there were 288 one-stop shops (*werkwinkels*) in 273 Flemish cities and municipalities. Due to rationalisation and efficiency processes, many have been forced to close during the last couple of years.

Collaboration with the private sector

VDAB offers several services directly to employers who require direct communication and strong engagement. There are contacts with private sector representative bodies and with large employers in order to develop the provision of training as well as other employment services.

Some schools work closely together with businesses in order to provide work experience to their students. Some technical and vocational schools have formal forms of collaboration with sectoral training funds (e.g. with regard to the construction sector). Regional Technological Centres represent an important area-based partnership at the local level between employers and public employment services – see Box 3.3.

Box 3.2. Regional Technological Centres (*Regionale Technologische Centra*)

Regional Technological Centres (RTC) create synergies between education and business to facilitate transitions from school to work, and to enhance the quality of technical and vocational education. Every five years, an agreement is made between these centres and the Flemish government based upon a strategic action plan, which include labour market information on the position of youth in the labour market.

The RTC covering the province of Antwerp makes high tech infrastructure and training accessible for all schools in the province. It promotes innovative techniques and methods and stimulates apprenticeships and work-based learning. The target audience is students in the third grade of full-time and part-time secondary education including those with special needs. The RTC is also involved in delivering some projects with one of the Antwerp Talent Houses (*Talentenfabriek*) and with VDAB.

RTC Limburg is providing innovative training as well as information about apprenticeships and work-based learning for students in schools in the Limburg region. This RTC targets students in the third grade of technical and vocational education (TSO and BSO) and their teachers. Besides the educational providers, this partnership includes industrial federations, sectoral training funds, employers, representatives of consultation platforms, representatives of higher education providers, VDAB and Syntra.

Collaboration between government departments

At the Flemish level, each policy department develops its own strategy taking into account developments in other policy domains or levels, or looking for synergies where possible. For example, the Department of Work and Social Economy works closely together with SERR and RESOC to develop integrated employment and socio-economic development policies. There is also regular inter-departmental collaboration between the Department of Work and Social Economy and between the Department of Education and Training, as well as with the Department of Welfare, Public Health and Family on economic and innovation policies.

Collaboration in the area of adult education

Joint strategies are also developed in the area of adult education, bringing together the providers of adult education within the educational system. With regard to adult education, Flanders is divided in 13 regions. In each region, a partnership is established between centres for adult education and centres for basic education to form a consortium.

For example, VOL-ANT is active in the City of Antwerp and 10 surrounding municipalities operating 14 centres for adult education and 1 centre for basic education. In Limburg, there are two consortia – one in the northern part of Limburg (consisting of 24 cities and municipalities, bringing together 11 centres for adult education and 1 centre for basic education), and one in the south (covering 20 cities and municipalities, bringing together 12 centres for adult education and 1 centre for basic education). A reform of the consortia is planned, including a restructuring of their overall organisation. It is possible that only 6 consortia will remain for the whole of the Flemish Community, representing educational providers.

Evidence based policy making

Employment policies and strategies are based on an analysis of available data. An important data source is the unemployment register of VDAB, which consists of individual records. Anyone registered with the unemployment system is recorded from the day of entry. In this database, it is possible to monitor whether an individual is unemployed. However, VDAB does not necessarily know whether someone who leaves the unemployment register went to employment or to some other situation, such as inactivity or old-age-pension.

With DIMONA-data, this problem can partly be solved. DIMONA requires that whenever a Belgian employer engages a new employee, they are legally obliged to immediately inform the social security agency in order to reduce informality. By combining information from VDAB with DIMONA, it is possible to know outcomes of job seekers. From 2007, DIMONA information has been added to the database of VDAB and updated on a monthly basis. Other data are gathered and synthesised to inform local programmes and strategies such as demographics, participation in training and education, as well as unqualified school leavers. New policies and programmes often reference results from different evaluations, which are generally funded by the Flemish government, sectoral bodies, provinces and cities.

In terms of evaluation, a caveat has to be made, in the sense that while VDAB has information about gross outflow results, it generally does not use a counterfactual design, meaning that they have limited information about net-effectiveness (e.g. the actual result for a given participant, compared to what the results would have been, if the participant would not have participated). Data on labour market outcomes from participation in employment and training programmes as well as student transitions could be improved. In particular, there is no data collected concerning individuals who participate in centres for adult education.

In Antwerp, the city produces comprehensive reports which compile quantitative and qualitative information about specific labour market sectors. These reports include data for the City of Antwerp as well as the surroundings areas. Indicators include characteristics of the student population, characteristics of jobseekers, number of employers, professions and vacancies, as well as education and training opportunities. If possible, trends are analysed to detect evolutions within sectors. The results of a survey of employers with regard to the need for generic and sector-specific competences are also included. This also includes an overview of policies at the European, federal, Flemish and regional level.

Labour market forecasting is not well developed in Flanders: forecasts often do not go beyond a time frame of three years, but awareness of the importance of forecasting is growing. The Flemish ESF Agency has launched two calls for detecting future skill and training needs targeting sectoral training funds and stimulating partnerships between sectors. Information about expected changes in recruitment needs is pursued by making optimal use of existing data. In depth sector studies are undertaken to reveal expected changes in jobs with the ultimate aim of increasing the transparency of the Flemish labour market, in order to focus investments in training and education programmes to labour market demands. The information obtained is often used for career guidance and the targeted activation of job seekers.

Data within travel to work areas

There is some fit between administrative boundaries and the local travel to work area. The fit is better for some sub-regions, such as neighbourhoods within Brussels. With regard to the city of Antwerp, the travel to work area is far bigger than the administrative area. The travel to work area is also not only situated within the province of Antwerp, but extends to the province of East-Flanders.

Theme 2: Adding value through skills

Flexible training open to all in a broad range of sectors

At local level, a wide range of training courses are available at different skills levels. As most of the education and training programmes are subsidised by the government, they are affordable to the majority of the residents. If course sizes are not sufficient, waiting lists are created before introducing a course, which usually does not take longer than six months. In general, there is a high level of institutional autonomy which leads to interesting and innovative training programmes.

Figure 3.3. **Local job creation dashboard: Adding value through skills**

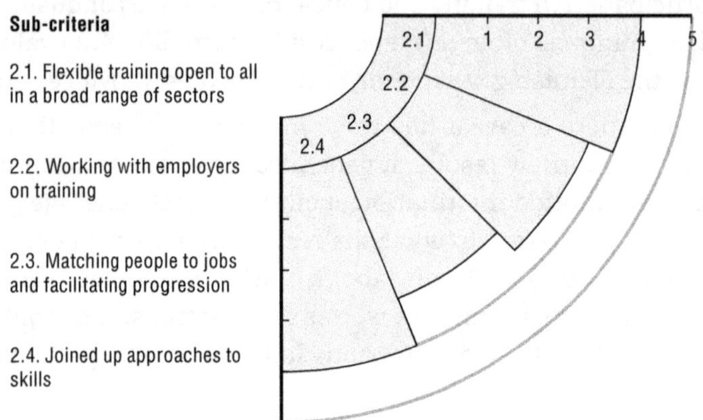

Previous OECD research has highlighted that the adult education system in Flanders is particularly strong with good geographical coverage and centres playing an important role as second chance providers offering basic skills programmes (Musset, 2013). VDAB and Syntra also offer a wide variety of training programmes tailored to the needs of individuals and employers, adapted to existing skill levels.

In Flanders, the qualifications framework developed in 2009 aims to make the system more coherent, by making qualifications more transparent and comparable across training providers, including centres for adult education, university colleges, and VDAB competence centres (Musset, 2013). Professional qualifications are in the process of being defined in terms of job competences. The COMPETENT system is developed and maintained by SERV linking with the Flemish Qualifications Framework, and in collaboration with experts from social partners, sectors and other stakeholders. Previous OECD research has noted that with the use of the eight levels of the Flemish Qualifications Framework and the description of jobs in terms of competences, it will become clearer which programmes lead to the same qualification level and to the same job (Musset, 2013).

All unemployed people have the option to participate in subsidised training provided by VDAB in a range of sectors, including construction, wood, electricity, ICT, health care, and commerce. People who are temporarily unemployed can also benefit from subsidised training recognised by VDAB. Job seekers participating in a recognised training programme are entitled to free training (e.g. no tuition), transportation allowances, as well as subsidised child care. Employed workers also have access to training, as well as subsidised options in the adult education system. Depending on the programme, eligibility criteria with regard to skills levels might be applied in order to avoid people participating in courses in which they are not qualified. All training providers provide an after-hours training option. Higher professional education (e.g. the level between secondary education and bachelor level) tends to be less flexible for learners because courses start at certain periods twice during the year.

Most vocational training covers generic skills, but also takes into account the specific skill needs and level of the individual (e.g. communication with co-workers or clients, and even networking). There are initiatives that are developed in collaboration between VDAB and providers within the educational system (e.g. secondary education, adult education and higher education) targeting job seekers.

For example, In Limburg, a one-year full-time training programme for industrial design has been developed by VDAB in partnership with Kunstschool Genk which is school for secondary and post-secondary education. The aim of the training is to: 1) develop vocational skills in the field of industrial design, 2) give students work-based experience through apprenticeship opportunities with employers, and 3) to develop entrepreneurship skills. The training leads to a certificate in Industrial Design and a certificate of Management. Employers are involved in the training programme, as well as VOKA – the local Chamber of Commerce. This post-secondary programme targets job seekers older than 22 years or who have left the educational system for at least two years, and who are able to participate in training in Dutch at the level of higher secondary education. No fees have to be paid. However, it should be noted that this type of collaboration with the educational system is not always evident and depends on local level relationships.

Working with employers on training

Employers who report that their demand for skilled workers is not met often point to the lack of adequate work attitudes and generic skills, and less to the lack of vocational skills. If they mention the lack of vocational skills, it is often in reference to skills not being up-to-date because trainees do not always work with the latest equipment and technology.

As SMEs are an important driver of growth within Flanders, training programmes specifically target these types of employers. SMEs may be granted up to 40 000 EUR per year in subsidies for, among other things, training, strategic advice and coaching. The amount that may be allocated to training within the overall subsidy is topped up at 2 500 EUR. Assistance is provided by VDAB, but also by sectoral training funds where specialised consultants are assigned to provide this type of assistance and support.

Comprehensive actions are taken to ensure that training meets the needs of local employers. Training is planned in consultation with employers and sector associations. The content of training is adapted to the job and competence profiles of each sector. If there are changes in employer demand, VDAB is able to modify courses to reflect the needs of industry. Employers are often involved in the development of training courses and there is close co-operation with providers, who have to prove that there is a demand for the training programmes they are going to deliver. Training is customised to the needs of local employers but the perceived value of certification by employers varies among programmes – something which is trying to be addressed through the Flemish qualifications framework.

Apprenticeships and work-based training opportunities

The development of more workplace training opportunities is an urgent issue within Flanders and efforts are being made to enhance the number of trainees in the workplace.

Box 3.3. **Sectoral Networks and Talent Houses (*Sectorale netwerken and Talentenhuizen*)**

In Antwerp, several sectoral networks have been established bringing together educational providers and labour market actors aimed at promoting smooth transitions from education to work. These sectoral networks are governed by the City of Antwerp and VDAB, who have signed a formal collaboration agreement. These agreements not only assign responsibility and divide tasks among the partners, but also include goals and targets to be reached.

A project manager is assigned to each sectoral network and experts are engaged. The financial means are provided by the City and by VDAB, and additional means are acquired through the European Social Fund. The networks are supported by sectoral organisations, sectoral training funds, social partners, educational providers, and regional technological centres. Each network establishes collaboration between stakeholders through a sectoral commission, a core group and thematic working groups. The aim is to develop action plans (for the short and long term), starting from a thorough analysis of the local educational system and the labour market.

A sectoral network can be converted to a Talent House when a sector is willing to invest in a partnership which requires a strong sectoral organisation; when the development of competences can be an answer to the recruitment problems (e.g. a Talent House is not the right answer when recruitment problems are to be attributed to the lack of job quality; and when the sector is of economic importance to the region. Four sectoral networks have been converted to Talent Houses: 1) Construction (Talentenwerf); 2) Industry (Talentenfabriek); 3) Harbour – Logistics (Talentenstroom); and 4) Education (Onderwijstalent).

Work-based learning is systematically used in VDAB programmes, however within programmes in centres for adult education, there is no formal requirement for work-based learning (Musset, 2013).

A number of initiatives have been recently launched to encourage greater workplace training. For example the regional technological centre in Antwerp collaborates with EANDIS (an energy distribution company) to provide individuals an opportunity to learn about the electricity and gas network. Teachers and trainers who would like to make use of this training centre follow a "train the trainer" model in order to provide the workplace training themselves, supported by EANDIS professionals.

In Limburg, Arcus Plus is a competence, expertise and innovation centre in the city of Maaseik, which provides up-to-date technological training to make teachers more competent with regard to didactical approaches. There is strong collaboration between schools and employers in this centre. Training provided is tailored to the needs of companies, and companies can use the equipment for their own employees after-school hours. Participants operating the centre include a secondary school, a centre for adult education and Syntra.

Matching people to jobs to quality jobs

Career planning for students is provided by centres for pupil guidance and financed by the Flemish government. One of their tasks is to support individuals with regard to their school careers. Specific initiatives are also available, such as the Job Market (*Jobmarkt*) organised in the city of Maaseik. Every year, a job market is held to bring together local companies and students. Approximately 600 students and 40 companies attended the job market in 2013. This type of initiative is quite common in other cities within the region of Flanders. Another project is the HorizonTaal, which is available in Limburg and Antwerp. It includes initiatives to support youth in secondary education to make informed career choices. Sectoral and regional development bodies contribute to this initiative, and the information available to students is based on local labour market sectors (e.g. logistics, and life sciences in the City of Antwerp).

The city of Antwerp has a career planning service to support schools, teachers and individuals (youth and adults). One of the instruments is *Studiewijzer* which is a website that provides information about study options for pupils and students in secondary and higher education, and also for adults in adult education. Universities offer careers advice geared to local industries through career fairs, but this is often limited to specific sectors.

Job Shops (*Werkwinkels*) provide information about the local labour market (e.g. which occupations and sectors are doing well) and about the associated education and training opportunities. Out-placement services are aimed at people who find themselves in a crisis situation of short-term dismissal. They are assisted in reflecting on their career and receive information about potential labour market opportunities to find a new job.

Every employed person (including the self-employed) is entitled to subsidised career planning support and may choose among several providers. This support is not only informational and practical, but focuses on career management including extensive reflection and motivation. This service is easily accessible and in the case of Limburg, employees facing job loss are being provided with extensive career planning advice and support to assist them in their next work transition following the closure of the Ford factory.

Job profiles are produced for several sectors at the Flemish and national level. 559 job profiles (*competent-fiches*) are available and kept up-to-date. The profiles are developed by the SERV in collaboration with the individual sectors. These profiles are publicly available in an electronic database. Training programmes offered by VDAB and vocational education institutions are adapted to these profiles. Many job profiles are adapted to the regional level. In Limburg, the Provincial Development Agency (*provinciale ontwikkelingsmaatschappij*) is in the process of commissioning a research project aimed at profiling the jobs in the logistics sector, and more specifically the jobs with hard-to-fill vacancies. For each of these jobs, required competences will be determined and articulated in the associated job profile.

Activation and job-matching

All unemployed people receive assistance from VDAB. Unemployed individuals who are deemed to have significant barriers are invited first for an individual consultation with local VDAB offices. Those individuals who require less intensive support can make use of on-line instruments, such as a database with vacancies. The idea is that many newly unemployed individuals will be able to find a job without intensive support. Therefore devoting a lot of attention to all new entrants is not considered to be cost-effective. This is also the case for training subsidised by VDAB. Many unemployed individuals are referred to training quite quickly, such as low-skilled youth, whereas others can make use of web-based training (languages, online ICT courses) during the first months of unemployment, where no instructor is involved in the training.

For job-matching, VDAB has a large database with vacancies which includes temporary and more permanent jobs. Matches between the vacancies and job seekers are made based on the competences, qualifications and the experience of the individual job seeker. This information can be consulted on-line and also in several public places (e.g. large shopping malls and public libraries). In addition, one of the main functions of the *Jobkanaal* project is to facilitate matching between vulnerable target groups and vacancies.

Locally, there are strategies and concrete actions to better match skills supply and demand, where sectors or employers are experiencing difficulties accessing skilled people. In Antwerp, the Educational Council (*Onderwijsraad Antwerpen*) have chosen to develop strategies to match skills supply and demand on a sectoral and regional level by discussing how schools and employers can work together. Actions are established with regard to situated competence-based learning and guidance.

Procedures for the validation of skills gained informally at work or in the education or training system have been introduced in Flanders. Procedures are established for more than 50 professions, in a broad range of sectors (commerce, construction, food industry, health care, the clothing industry, and life sciences). Assessments are standardised making use of job and competence profiles and assessment centres are designated for each profession.

Joined up approaches to skills

Economic development stakeholders consider the need to retain and attract talent and this is done in different ways. The provincial development agency of Limburg has commissioned research projects with regard to the labour market in the Euregio Maas-Rijn. A SWOT analysis is being carried out to determine the reasons for brain drain to other regions, the number of pupils, students and adults with relevant education and skills, as well as the number of job seekers with relevant job aspirations and qualifications.

Joined up local approaches to skills are common and the focus is on co-ordination using formal agreements across several different policy sectors. These agreements are supported by the Department of Work and Social Economy. Collaboration with local key actors is essential, and it is expected that local approaches will create value because local governments can create synergies between different policy domains.

Since 2007, a local education policy (*Lokaal flankerend onderwijsbeleid*) supports actions by the local government in the area of education. Cities develop a policy plan and their projects are eligible for subsidies from the Flemish government. It gives cities the opportunity to develop policy actions geared at the local situation and experiment with new innovative policies.

Antwerp, Genk and Hasselt have developed local educational plans and received subsidies for several projects. For example, in Antwerp, the "learning and work" project provided work experience to young people under the age of 25 who are still in education. Partners in the project included seven centres for learning and working, Syntra, centres for pupil guidance, schools (TISO, TIVO), a representative body of entrepreneurs (UNIZO), the Chamber of Commerce, RESOC, VDAB, and several not for profit organisations targeting groups at-risk.

Since 2011, Excellent Centres (*Excellente centra*) are a type of collaboration between sectors and key actors with regard to labour market policy, education and training. A sectoral approach is used, starting with an analysis of employment and skill needs with the aim of reducing the number of hard-to-fill vacancies.

Box 3.4. **The City of Antwerp – Work and Economy Department**

The Work and Economy department is working on Antwerp's socioeconomic planning and development, mainly focusing on attracting new investors, facilitating start-ups and stimulating competitiveness for growth and employment. Through several projects and initiatives, the department is dedicated to creating a diverse and strong economic environment where efficiency and profitability go hand in hand with sustainability and social responsibility. The Agency consists of various teams:

1. The Business Strategy and Innovation team focuses on economic strategy making the City of Antwerp as business-friendly as possible. The teams support the development of city projects with an economic focus such as the industrial site of Blue Gate Antwerp, incubator BlueChem, and Start-up City.
2. The Investment desk offers customised advice and support to investors and market players who wish to invest in the city. Location guidance is provided where a location manager helps entrepreneurs in their search for a location that matches their needs. The team also actively promotes the re-development of empty business and commercial premises. Licensing guidance (guidance for the licenses needed by entrepreneurs and directing to the appropriate city department is another key service).
3. The Retail and Hotels, Restaurants and Catering team reinforces the city's shopping and hospitality areas by supporting and advising how to start a business in hospitality, investing in the street view of commercial centres, and developing and supporting city projects with retail or hospitality focus
4. The Business Desk is the contact point for new and established businesses, as well as for the self-employed. The Business Desk provides information on permits issued by the City of Antwerp as well as the application of a renovation subsidy for commercial properties.
5. The Business Promotion team focuses on promoting Antwerp as a city "open for business" in business press and publishing and through conferences and networking events
6. The Work and Social Economy team offers customised services for filling vacancies and demand-oriented training. It co-ordinates the sectoral networks (hospitality, care) and the Talent houses as well as the development of actions to tackle youth employment.

The initiatives and projects are developed in collaboration with the VDAB, organisations for social welfare, other city departments (education, youth), representatives of economic sectors, other labour market actors and education-training providers.

Theme 3: Targeting policy to local employment sectors and investing in quality jobs

Relevance of provision to important local employment sectors and global trends and challenges

In Flanders it is common practice that employment programmes and initiatives are geared to important local employment sectors, especially in cities and in regions confronted with specific difficulties. The sectoral approach through the Talent Houses in Antwerp (as described in Box 3.3) are a good example as are the priorities defined in the Strategic Action Plan in Limburg (described earlier on pg. 23). In Limburg, important local employment sectors are logistics, life sciences, business services and ICT, construction and the care economy, clean technology, food (fruit), and tourism.

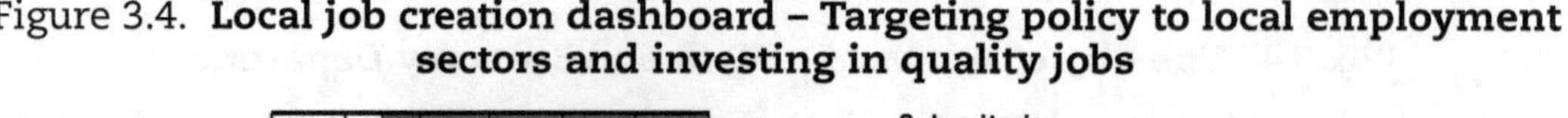

Figure 3.4. **Local job creation dashboard – Targeting policy to local employment sectors and investing in quality jobs**

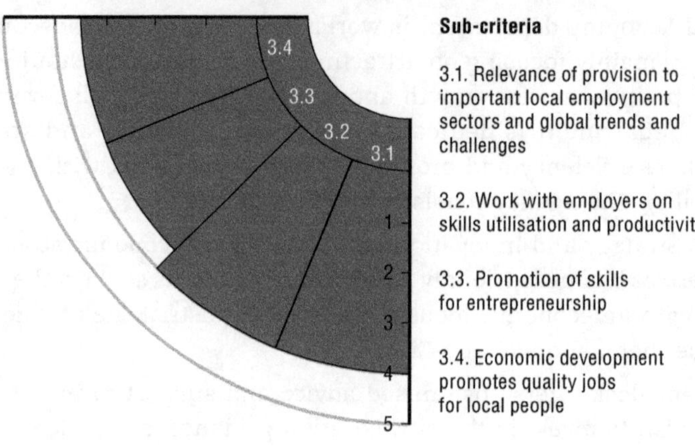

It is common practice to gear the provision of training programmes to developments in the labour market. New adult training and VET courses are for instance geared to new types of employment especially in the care sector and green employment. A recent example was the development of training courses on solar energy. The rise in employment in this sector was due to specific governmental measures such as subsidies for households to install solar energy systems.

Talentenwerf is a Talent House in the field of construction which brings together VDAB, the City of Antwerp, the Educational Council of Antwerp, education and training providers, and the sectoral training fund of FVB-Constructiv. Other partners include the labour unions and sectoral federations. This network is also supported by the Flemish government with the aim to match people to jobs that will be generated by the large construction and infrastructure works in the City of Antwerp. An important feature of this Talent House is that the services are provided by a team of experts, using the expertise and tools of VDAB targeted to employers, educational providers, students and their parents as well as job seekers, which facilitates the development and co-ordination of actions.

In 2013, almost 900 individuals came to *Talentenwerf*. Four out of five were interested in participating in training courses; one out of five was looking for a job in the construction sector. Job seekers are presented to employers, who were then invited to get in touch with the job seekers directly. The *Talentenwerf* team looks for "hidden" vacancies, which are vacancies that are not advertised by employers. In the near future, the support for job seekers will be intensified and the aim is to reach more employers. Over the past five years, one out of four job seekers who came to *Talentenwerf* found a job and is still working in the construction sector.

To support the transition to a low-carbon economy it is necessary to invest in appropriate skills, knowledge and competences. The OECD is also conducting a complementary study in Flanders which will examine the specific skills needed to support economic growth that is green and inclusive. It examines how efforts by public policies, education and training systems and the private sector can be accelerated to support progress towards green growth in different industrial sectors, and to ease the transition to greener jobs. A mixture of transversal and specific skills are needed by different industry clusters, and the project will investigate how flexible and responsive the education and labour market system is to developing those skills that are needed to meet business objectives, both now and in the future.

Work with employers on skills utilisation and productivity

Employers who want to improve introduce strategies for their staff's development and employability skills can receive financial support from the Flemish Department of Work and Social Economy as well as from dedicated 'diversity consultants' through diversity and career plans. In 2012, 890 business and organisations submitted such a diversity and career plan.

Several programmes and services are available, with regard to skills utilisation and work organisation. The toolbox called "sustainable employment" developed by the Foundation Innovation and Labour (*Stichting Innovatie en Arbeid*) collects examples of initiatives in the field of sustainable employment, combining skills utilisation and work organisation and disseminates tools to be used to create sustainable employment. The tools as well as a description of several good practices are publicly available. Both VKW and VOKA (the local chambers of commerce) publish information emphasising the importance of continuously improving work organisation, inviting key note speakers to discuss this topic during events and organising workshops about the importance of the issue.

With regard to work organisation, Flanders Synergy (which operates under a public-private co-operation structure) became an important actor providing support to enterprises to innovate their work organisation. The aim is to create adaptive organisations, and meaningful and sustainable jobs. Services for employers are subsidised by the Flemish government. Flanders Synergy has an advisory board, which includes academic researchers, social partners including unions, enterprises and consultants.

Job coaching is a service provided by VDAB. An employer who has hired persons belonging to an at-risk group (e.g. migrants, older workers, disabled people, low-skilled people, ex-prisoners) can ask to be supported by a job coach. Job coaches help the new employee to develop motivation, adequate attitudes and behaviour. The aim is to ensure sustainable employment and this service is provided to employers for free.

Another good example is *Jobkanaal* which was initiated by VOKA, UNIZO, VERSO and VKW (all employer organisations) and is supported by the Flemish government. Partners are VDAB, SLN (Support for local networks, the umbrella organisation of several non-profit providers of social programmes), VVSG (Flemish Cities and Municipalities, the umbrella organization of Flemish cities and municipalities) and GTB (specialised guidance centres for persons with a handicap). *Jobkanaal* consists of advisors, who facilitate the recruitment of vulnerable groups, and provide HR-policy advice taking into account labour market developments.

In 2010, The Platform Care Limburg was introduced and supported by the province. The aim was to develop common policy for the care sector, to co-ordinate actions and to build up expertise. Innovation in work organisation is a core theme of the platform. Examples are the restructuring of labour processes and opportunities for flexible work organisation. One of the innovations is to create full-time jobs, combining part-time jobs across organisations with the expected outcome of increased labour productivity.

Involvement of education and training institutes in local applied research

Universities and research centres are often asked to undertake applied research of relevance to the local economy. The research deals with many topics, such skills forecasting, employment indicators, project development, and evaluation. Research projects are commissioned by sectors, by the cities or regions themselves, or by the Flemish government. Research projects can also be undertaken to support local firms.

Box 3.5. Practice labs for innovative work organisation

In Limburg, "Practice labs for innovative work organisation" have been set up to work with businesses, as part of a broader programme developed due to concerns about demographic change and an ageing workforce (50plusdatwerkt). The ACV union has played a key role in establishing and implementing the initiative.

The practice labs have been set up in the construction, logistics, healthcare, social economy, social service/care and agricultural sectors. Separate labs were established for each sector but in practice, labs can work with mixed groups, and can support both large and small firms. Eight workshops have taken place in 2013/14, each involving 6-8 companies. A consultant was hired to work on the workshops. They function as a learning network where companies share experience. Managers are encouraged to consider where they can effect change to make sure that workers have more involvement in the way that the firm operates. Each lab covers seven themes, each of which is a different area where the manager can have an influence. One theme, for example, has been exploring new ways that firms can expand their market base to improve the quality of their organisation (in terms of efficiency, flexibility, quality, innovation, sustainability) while also improving job quality.

Supervisors play the role of coach and act as a sounding board for participants who have questions, both within and outside of the lab sessions. Participants receive assignments to translate theory into practice when they return to the workplace. The construction sector has now started to run their own independent workshops. Unions report that the workshops have improved their relationships with local employers.

Furthermore, academic researchers are often asked to participate in projects through membership of an expert group or the board of organisations contributing to the development of the local economy.

Promotion of skills for entrepreneurship

There are public employment programmes provided by VDAB that encourage entrepreneurship in Syntra and Starterslabo. Job seekers are screened based on their business ideas and if approved, they are assisted in starting their own business. Support is provided to develop a business plan and participants are provided with relevant mentorship and entrepreneurship education opportunities.

A vocational training programme (in secondary education as well as in adult education) can be complemented with a management course. This course is often optional, but sometimes it is an essential part of the programme. Adults who are not in the education or training system can participate in these courses. Within the dual system, the training provided by Syntra Flanders is geared towards entrepreneurship skills.

Entrepreneurship skills are part of specific university programmes mainly related to economics, engineering and applied sciences, sometimes as part of the core curriculum, sometimes as an option. However, awareness is raised for entrepreneurship skills in other domains (health sciences, educational sciences, food and agriculture).

A specific barrier to the development of entrepreneurship is that in Flanders "entrepreneurship" often has a negative connotation. Very often, "entrepreneurship" is also interpreted in a limited way (e.g. starting your own business while it can also refer to utilising entrepreneurship skills while working for a company or a not for profit organisation) or in a negative way (e.g. after failure of a business).

Antwerp created "enterprise centres" (*bedrijvencentra*) which assist start-ups and young entrepreneurs in developing sustainable businesses. Within these centres, several companies within similar sectors are located in the same place (e.g. design and creative professions, construction, high tech). "We are chemisty" is a project organised in collaboration with the sectoral federation and the municipal body for Harbour Antwerp (*Gemeentelijk Havenbedrijf Antwerpen*). The aim is to motivate students to choose a career in the life sciences sector.

Economic development promotes quality jobs for local people

Flanders Investment and Trade plays an active role supporting home-based companies doing business abroad and foreign companies looking to invest or expand operations within Flanders. Strategies promoting quality jobs for local people often include active marketing of the local labour force to potential inward investors. An important role is played by the Provincial Development Agency (*Provinciale Ontwikkelingsmaatschappij*) and by cities.

When POM Limburg promotes the region, it provides information with regard to human capital, referring to the demographic composition of the labour force, the qualification levels, language skills as well as the opportunities provided by the presence of educational and training institutions. The collaboration between universities and enterprises is often promoted and sometimes, financial support for new employers (e.g. in the form of loans at low rates) is provided to attract them to the region.

In Antwerp, the city emphasises the presence of a high skilled and multilingual labour force and refers to the presence of universities and institutes for higher education. Specific competences are mentioned such as creativity and information about the domains covered by education providers is also available.

The quality and quantity of jobs offered by local inward investors is taken into consideration in the planning process. New enterprises for instance have to comply with certain rules before receiving permits, and often a dialogue is started with new enterprises in order to create commitment with regard to the local labour force. An important feature of Limburg's inward investment strategy is that efforts are made to attract enterprises that create jobs for blue-collar workers as well. Limburg wants to attract large enterprises but also wants to be attractive to smaller enterprises, in order to diminish dependency from a small number of very large employers.

New local construction and development activities are considered to be opportunities for education and employment. A good and recent example can be found in Limburg where the Strategic Action Plan Limburg (SALK) (as described earlier on pg. 23) emphasises the importance of new local construction and development activities to provide new employment opportunities to the population such as the development of tourism (recreation and infrastructure); exploitation of former mines (Be-mine, Terhills, Thor-park); the development of a fashion incubator; and construction of social housing.

Antwerp is not confronted with job destruction. Rather, huge public construction works (traffic works aimed at improving mobility in the Antwerp region) planned to be executed between 2016-22 and will also create new jobs. In public procurement, tenderers are often asked to fulfil specific requirements (e.g. to make use of the workforce in the social economy), but the possibilities for procurement to source quality jobs is limited due to legal restrictions.

Theme 4: Being inclusive

Employment and training programmes are geared to local "at risk" groups

In general, employment programmes specifically target certain at-risk groups but some groups are under-represented in the participation of many services. The take-up of services is monitored in a limited way. The Flemish social partners diversity commission (*Commissie Diversiteit*) has asked for an evaluation of the effectiveness of some employment measures in order to enhance monitoring quality and introduce a systematic process for monitoring outcomes across regions.

Figure 3.5. **Local Job Creation Dashboard – Being inclusive**

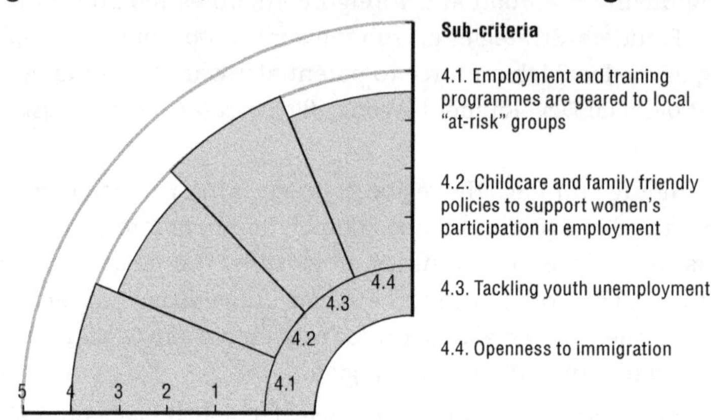

Training programmes recognised by VDAB (for instance, within adult education institutions) charge reduced fees to job seekers in order to make them more accessible (training at VDAB's competence centres remain free for jobseekers). There are a range of language training programmes that are available in order to make VET and adult training more accessible for those individuals who do not speak Dutch or have low literacy levels. There is a VET offer for specific groups at risk including prisoners (training and guidance provided by VDAB); and people with disabilities (transport allowances paid by VDAB). Literacy training is provided on demand in collaboration with organisations targeting groups at risk, such as migrant women and OCMW clients. One of the tasks of VDAB is to create jobs/job placements for people not ready to enter formal employment. Disabled people receive special guidance and there are specific measures including subsidies to make it easier for employers to hire them.

Outreach activities

VET and adult training institutions participate in outreach activities, and some training programmes are delivered directly in disadvantaged communities. Youth organisations are most often situated in disadvantaged communities and work closely with the neighbourhood and community. Other adult training institutions do not really target groups at risk, and are as such not consistently participating in area-based approaches. However, this does not mean they do not pay attention to the needs of disadvantaged students. Often, special support is available to these students. Social economy projects providing training or work experience are also very often situated in disadvantaged neighbourhoods. VDAB Antwerp has set up several outreach pilots for unemployed people who are not in contact with the employment service, especially unemployed youth and ethnic minorities.

Box 3.6. Werkhaven and the "key carriers"-project

Werkhaven Antwerp is a non-profit association, more specifically a social economy company and a "daughter" of the city of Antwerp, called an "EVA" (externally autonomous agency). There are about 320 people working for the organisation. It targets persons unemployed for more than one year, have a low level of education and more than 85% of them have a foreign origin.

The "key carriers" project is an innovative activity, which above all brings together the target group workers and the citizens. Individuals and organisations can ask the city department "Living Together" for a meeting room in a public building for work or personal functions. The department suggests a meeting room and the user can count on a key carrier of Werkhaven in order to open and close the room. Under this programme, a school for example, does not need to keep staff working in order to open and close the college gym for a sports association. Besides opening and closing, the key carriers have an important role in logistical support and social control. They help by organising the room, setting up chairs, making coffee and keep an eye on the way the rooms are left for the next day or group.

Taking into account all these tasks, the key carriers have a big responsibility and need to have a specific profile. Presently, there are more than 50 rooms managed under this programme, which have all their own access modalities and properties. Key carriers must be flexible, customer friendly and independent. Many older workers participate in the programme, which reflects the situation in Flanders where older workers have less possibilities to participate in the regular labour market.

Informal and illegal employment

Most measures against informal and illegal employment are related to control and sanctioning. However, since 2003 there is a system of service vouchers (*dienstencheques*) available throughout Flanders that is also helping people out of informal and illegal employment. The aim of the system was to create new jobs by subsidising household tasks (individual households pay a reduced fee, while government bridges the difference between that fee and the employee's gross wage). The system is very successful in reaching workers and households, and evaluations have demonstrated that it is effective in fostering employment.

Childcare and family friendly policies to support women's participation in employment

Most families can access affordable and subsidised child care, but the demand is not fully met. There is subsidised pre-school child care available throughout Flanders with prices from EUR 1.50-27.30/day depending on the income of the family, the amount of hours the child is in formal care and the number of other children within the family. VDAB provides child care subsidies to cover the costs for children of unemployed persons who follow approved training courses. Local initiatives are taken to make childcare accessible for disadvantaged groups. The City of Antwerp for instance has created and financed special places for child care that are available short-term for parents who were unemployed but have recently found a job.

In 2012, there were 38.7 formal preschool child care places per 100 children between the ages of 0-2 years. This conceals important provincial differences comparing Antwerp and Limburg (33.2 and 32.2 places respectively per child between 0-2 years) to the other provinces (East-Flanders: 41.3, West-Flanders: 44.8, Flemish-Brabant: 41.2). The yearly report of "Kind en Gezin" of 2012 notes that 63 709 preschool formal child care places with a fee that is dependent on the family income and 26 017 places for which the fee is not dependent on family income. Therefore, most but not all of the preschool child care places (71.0%) are thus determined based on family income.

In April 2012, the Flemish Government adopted a decree which among others incorporates the explicit goal of having 50 child care places per 100 children younger than three years by 2016, and child care should be available to any family that has a need by 2020. One study conducted on this issue suggests that increasing the number of formal pre-school child care places would still lead to an increase in total labour supply as families switch to formal child care although some households would also reduce working hours (Vanleenhove, 2013).

Early years education

Affordable early years education is broadly available. In the Flemish region, a rule has been put into place stating that in order for a child to enter elementary education, he or she should have participated in kindergarten ("early childhood education") for at least 220 days. The government wants to increase participation in early childhood education. One survey found that 89.6% of the children in between the age of 2.5-3 years attend preschool at least part time (Hedebouw and Peetermans, 2009). This is in line with the figures of the Starting Strong II study which cites 90% for participation at the age of 2.5 years (OECD, 2006). Participation is free, including use of all items necessary to attain the developmental goals that are put forward by the government.

Schemes are in place to target increased participation in early years education among disadvantaged groups. Most of the places in formal preschool child care are dependent on the family income, making prices less of a threshold for participation. Hedebouw and Peetermans (2009) suggest that although the use of preschool childcare has increased over the years since 2002 in families with a mother of foreign origin, it does not significantly increase for disadvantaged families.

Kind en Gezin (Child and Family) places an emphasis on measures to increase child care use in families with a mother of foreign origin and in poor and disadvantaged families. Several pilot projects have been set-up (for example projects aimed at increasing inclusive child care through so called Centres for Child Care [*Centra voor Kinderopvang*]). Neighbourhood based child care facilities are being developed that work together with other local actors to reach less privileged families. However, for now, only 0.2 places in such care facilities are available for every 100 children between the ages of 0-2 years.

Care for the elderly

When it comes to the presence of affordable and subsidised care for the elderly, a distinction has to be made between care at home and residential care. Care at home is provided by not for profit organisations. All care provided by recognised services is subsidised, but elderly have to pay a small share (e.g. 5.44 EUR/hour or 6 EUR/hour for different types of domestic help) (Pacolet, De Coninck & De Wispelaere, 2013). There are no waiting lists with care being provided almost immediately upon request. Residential care is very diverse and provided by welfare services (OCMW), private not for profit organisations and commercial providers.

Family friendly policies

Data for Flanders show that 27.7% of the working population has made use of working time reduction options such as part time work or career breaks. Worker oriented flexibility, such as working from home or a four-day full time schedule are opted for by 18.1% of the working population, men and women equally. It is, however, offered to 41.8% of workers. Family friendly policies are not universally accepted or promoted by employers' organisations.

A traditional norm of a full time working week with over time work prevails so that a reduction of working time implies sacrificing career opportunities. Trade unions offer checklists for family friendly policies at the workplace, primarily directed to workers. An important family representation group (*Gezinsbond*) set up a charter on family friendly policies for companies. These initiatives are not widely adopted by employers, except for organisations in the public sector, such as local governments and health care institutions, and organisations with large networks, such as banks and insurance companies.

In sector or national level discussions, the bottlenecks seems to be the lack of legal control by trade unions over flexibility measures, and the limited margin of flexibility of employers in reorganising work, referring to the nature of the work and examples of women, as a rule, who managed to make careers either through sacrificing family life or successfully combining duties in work and private life.

Tackling youth unemployment

School dropouts and NEETs are a big source of concern for the government and all organisations involved in employment, education and training. An important new initiative is the Action Plan for Early School Leaving (*Actieplan Voortijdig Schoolverlaten*). The plan was developed at the Flemish level with specific tasks and initiatives to be carried out locally. A data warehouse will be constructed in order to provide localities with detailed information concerning the number of early school leavers. Schools and their educational umbrella organisations, Syntra, VDAB, and other organisations will be assigned tasks to process the information.

Since many years, policies and programmes have been developed to support NEETS, especially in bigger cities. The identification of these young people and active outreach are important parts of these strategies. In Antwerp, a central helpdesk for youth at risk was established in 2003. This helpdesk has the objective of reducing the number of school drop-outs. A system for early detection of problems has been developed and youth at risk are guided by several organisations in close collaboration with schools. Schools, centres for pupil guidance, welfare services, and police can report young people living in a very disadvantaged situation including domestic violence, showing risky behaviour as well as having behavioural problems. More than 7 000 youth have been registered in the last 10 years.

The professionals working for the Central Helpdesk develop tools to reduce and prevent school drop-outs. They also are responsible for monitoring and profiling youth as well as evaluating the interventions. The team is developing evidence-based policy measures and protocols.

In Limburg, a network called Right to Learn was established in 2013 to provide services for youth with truancy or other school problems, at risk of early school leaving. Educational providers and centres for pupil guidance, supported by many other partners (e.g. welfare and special care services) are collaborating to guarantee the right to learn for these individuals. Empowerment and social integration are core objectives, and parents will be actively involved whenever possible. If necessary, alternatives for school (at least during a short period) will be available. Presently evidence is being analysed, an inventory of good practices is made and a networking model is being developed. The possibility of creating a central register is being examined and the network is planned to be fully functional in 2015.

A new initiative in Flanders is the work experience for youth programme (*Werkinleving voor jongeren* – WIJ!), which subsidise projects targeted to 13 Flemish cities, including in the City of Antwerp and Limburg regions. A call was launched and proposals were submitted by organisations working in these cities – see Box 3.7.

Box 3.7. **Work experience for youth (*Werkinleving voor jongeren* WIJ!)**

Target group: unqualified young people (under 25 years) who are not employed, who are very difficult to integrate in the labour market (but who do not suffer from specific problems making specialised guidance necessary) and who are not supported yet. Allocation of the young people towards WIJ is guaranteed by the VDAB.

Scope: In Antwerp, more than 1 700 young people will be supported in a two year period. In Genk and Hasselt, approximately 200 young people will be supported. For the whole of Limburg, over 310 young people will be supported with the aim to lead young people to employment or to make them more skilled.

Services available: Individual vocational training (Individuele beroepsopleiding, IBO), apprenticeship through the federal apprenticeship system (Federale instapstages), vocational training provided by the PES (Competentieversterking bij VDAB), training "work experience for young people" (Werkinleving voor jongeren) and language training. Other services are job hunting and brokering, and the certification of competences. Individual guidance as well as group programmes are available. Employers do not pay for the apprenticeship, but they are expected to give apprentices the opportunity to reach the learning aims, to designate a mentor and to contribute to the evaluation of the apprentice.

Development support: for specific target groups it includes training with regard to vocational competences, but special attention is paid to generic competences and attitudes.

Organisations involved: private organisations, providers of supported employment, non-profit training and guidance organisations targeting groups at risk. The organisation providing the guidance is obliged to collaborate with the local government.

Openness to immigration

Recognition of educational qualifications acquired abroad is a service provided by NARIC. This service is free for many people (e.g. job seekers receiving guidance from VDAB), although some categories have to pay for the service. Skills obtained outside the academic educational system can be recognised.

Within the educational system, procedures for the recognition of acquired competences are developed. These procedures are accessible to all so migrants can also ask for the recognition of their skills, in order to gain access to the educational system, or in order to be able to choose the short track in education. Support for going through the procedures is available, but the recognition of qualifications acquired abroad is not always considered to be efficient.

Language training is widely available in education and training centres, as well as in the workplace. Language training is available in a wide range of subsidised services suited for all skills levels. In order to determine skill levels, immigrants are screened. Language training in the workplace is also available targeted to specific occupations in a broad range of sectors. An example of language training in the workplace provided by VDAB is NODW (*Nederlands op de werkvloer* – Dutch at the workplace). This type of course is promoted by several sectoral bodies. However, specific problems still have to be tackled when it comes to providing this type of training. For example, it is difficult to combine vocational education and training with language training.

General actions are in place aimed at raising awareness about labour market discrimination. There is a Flemish action plan to combat employment related discrimination (*Actieplan Bestrijding Arbeidsgerelateerde Discriminatie, ABAD*), which combines a prevention and sanctioning appoach. The plan will be evaluated annually and several professionals are assigned the task to tackle discrimination in the labour market (e.g. diversity consultants within unions and consultants within the sectoral training funds).

References

Bogaerts, K. et al. (2011), "Building Flexibility and Accountability Into Local Employment Services: Country Report for Belgium", *OECD Local Economic and Employment Development (LEED) Working Papers*, No. 2011/11, OECD Publishing, Paris, *http://dx.doi.org/10.1787/5kg3mkv0448s-en.*

Froy, F., S. Giguère and M. Meghnagi (2012), "Skills for Competitiveness: A Synthesis Report", *OECD Local Economic and Employment Development (LEED) Working Papers*, No. 2012/09, OECD Publishing, Paris, *http://dx.doi.org/10.1787/5k98xwskmvr6-en.*

Froy, F. et al. (2011), "Building Flexibility and Accountability Into Local Employment Services: Synthesis of OECD Studies in Belgium, Canada, Denmark and the Netherlands", *OECD Local Economic and Employment Development (LEED) Working Papers*, No. 2011/10, OECD Publishing, Paris, *http://dx.doi.org/10.1787/5kg3mkv3tr21-en.*

Giguère, S. and F. Froy (eds.) (2009), "Flexible Policy for More and Better Jobs", *Local Economic and Employment Development* (LEED), OECD Publishing, *http://dx.doi.org/10.1787/9789264059528-en.*

Hedebouw, G. and A. Peetermans (2009), *Het gebruik van opvang voor kinderen jonger dan 3 jaar in het Vlaams Gewest: eindrapport.* SWVG-Rapport (07). Leuven: Steunpunt Welzijn, Volksgezondheid en Gezin.

OECD (2013a), *OECD Economic Surveys: Belgium 2013*, OECD Publishing, Paris, *http://dx.doi.org/10.1787/eco_surveys-bel-2013-en.*

OECD (2013b), *Education at a Glance 2013: OECD Indicators*, OECD Publishing, *http://dx.doi.org/10.1787/eag-2013-en.*

OECD (2006), *Starting Strong II: Early Childhood Education and Care*, OECD Publishing, *http://dx.doi.org/10.1787/9789264035461-en.*

Pacolet, J., A. De Coninck and F. De Wispelaere (2013), *Financiering van de thuiszorg: het perspectief van de voorzieningen. Leuven: Steunpunt Welzijn*, Volkgsgezondheid en Gezin.

Chapter 4

Towards an action plan for jobs in Flanders, Belgium: Recommendations and best practices

Stimulating job creation at the local level requires integrated actions across employment, training and economic development portfolios. Co-ordinated place-based policies can help workers find suitable jobs, while also contributing to demand by stimulating productivity. This requires flexible policy management frameworks, information, and integrated partnerships which leverage the efforts of local stakeholders. This chapter outlines the key recommendations emerging from the OECD review of local job creation policies in Flanders, Belgium.

Better aligning programmes and policies to local economic development

Recommendation: Build on the high level of flexibility within employment services and continue to build partnerships and horizontal accountability mechanisms, which promote growth and employment. This can be done by identifying the best collaboration models which have led to strong policy integration and co-ordination.

Previous OECD research examined the level of flexibility within the employment service in Flanders and concluded that more flexibility was needed to give local employment offices a greater leadership role in formulating strategies and partnerships which tackle issues related to labour market activation, employment, economic development and inclusion (Bogaerts et al., 2011). Recent reforms introduced within VDAB have sought to equip local employment service managers with more discretion in the implementation of employment policies, which is a welcome development. Furthermore, giving local offices budget flexibility to design programmes in partnership with other actors will reduce duplication and create synergies in policy delivery.

Following the crisis, partnerships are a key governance tool to better connect the supply and demand of skills to ensure greater economic growth and productivity. This study has highlighted good examples of local collaboration among agencies and local governments. VDAB has many partnership agreements involving a plethora of networks and organisations, which contributes to a situation of relative institutional density. Within Antwerp, the Employment and Economic Development department of the city is a good example of a governance unit established within a local area to co-ordinate actions, which promote job creation, skills, and employment. If it does not already exist, other cities in Flanders could learn from this organisational structure as a best practice in organising local development efforts. There is also a level of horizontal accountability, which has been established between VDAB and the City of Antwerp, which should be replicated across other regions in Flanders.

Going forward, it is important that the government explore how to further reduce policy silos locally through horizontal governance arrangements. For example, if organisations are collaborating in Flanders, often, a co-ordinator has to be appointed from one of the organisations, which represents a separate resource for collaboration. Sometimes, this can impact the nature of collaboration because the co-ordinator will primarily represent the interests of their own organisation, as opposed to the overall partnership. Feedback from local stakeholders consulted for this study also point to the benefits that could achieved by having an intermediary organisation that can lead co-ordination among the relevant actors.

There is an opportunity for the Flemish government to explore collaboration models which overcome the financial and legal issues that come with working together. The Flemish government should explore how best to finance partnerships which encourage information sharing about employment outcomes across organisations. One option would be to allocate funding through strategic objectives, while allowing local partnerships to collaboratively identify targets and outcomes that will be delivered. Local organisations and agencies already benefit from strong local networking therefore the Flemish government should also examine how to streamline local governance arrangements to fit with broader travel to work areas.

Efforts to encourage joined-up working through shared funding can also improve policy adaptability and ensure programmes reflect local circumstances. While much effort has been made to inject flexibility into the employment system, the Flemish government will need to continue exploring how employment and skills policies are designed to reflect local circumstances. Local areas, such as Antwerp and Limburg can be the first to feel new developments in the labour market and identify emerging issues. Therefore, it is important that vertical accountability structures encourage dialogue between provincial and local organisations to quickly identify and respond to emerging issues, which might not be adequately addressed through existing programme envelopes.

The WIRED initiative from the United States provides a good example of a programme introduced to offset potential issues related to collaboration at the local and regional level. While the initiative has been disbanded, the social capital that was developed from networking among organisations remains an important outcome of the programme within the United States (see Box 4.1).

Box 4.1. **Resources for collaboration – example from the United States**

WIRED (Workforce Innovation in Regional Economic Development) was an initiative of the US. Department of Labor for the purpose of fostering collaboration among key stakeholders in designated regions and encouraging other activities in order to achieve the following goals:

- Regional Economic Development: Fueling regional economic competitiveness
- Regional Collaboration: Creating highly networked communities that are key to supporting innovation and the economic growth process
- Workforce System Transformation: Developing an integrated approach to workforce and economic development and education
- High-Skill High-Wage Jobs: Expanding employment and advancement opportunities for workers and catalysing the creation of high-skill and high-wage opportunities
- Disadvantaged Populations: Expanding opportunities to increase the work skills and work readiness of low-wage workers.

The US Department of Labor selected 39 regions through a competitive grant process. Each successful region was given up to 15 million USD over a three-year period with an overall outlay of 325 million USD. Each WIRED region determined their own regional boundaries, set their own specific objectives, developed their own strategies and implemented initiatives to meet those objectives based upon their understanding of their assets, challenges and opportunities. Typically, WIRED regions chose specific objectives that aligned workforce investment, economic development, and educational initiatives. Each region could use the grant funding to support their initiatives, and they were expected to leverage those funds with other private and government sources.

Source: OECD (2014e), *Employment and Skills Strategies in the United States*, OECD Reviews on Local Job Creation, OECD Publishing.

Recommendation: Continue to collect and share information and data about "what works" locally, including effective approaches to respond to the hiring needs of employers.

Information and evidence play a critical role in bringing local stakeholders together. The ability for local actors and partnerships to identify and respond to the barriers that some people face in getting into employment is shaped by the availability of adequate, timely local level data. Local data can also stimulate effective local partnerships, acting as a catalyst for action (Froy and Giguère, 2010). Authoritative and updated skills profiles of local labour markets are important in framing providers' strategies and strengthening accountability and can also galvanise local actors into a common agenda for action when used well.

While the collation of data at the sub-national level is strong in Flanders, there is room to improve its interpretation and use in policy-making and programme planning. In Flanders, most analysis is done on past and current trends but analysis on future trends is not comprehensively undertaken, which limits strategic local planning capacity. There are industry bodies which do sector studies, but these are done only for certain sectors and do not necessarily contain an analysis of local impacts. There is a need to continue the work of the existing Policy Research Centre and ensure it focuses on building evidence related to issues that are identified by local actors. The Flemish government could also further develop longitudinal tracking of individuals after course or programme completion. This is not easy to achieve however, with few OECD countries having a successful tracking system in place. Collecting quality data and using it effectively when designing, implementing and evaluating policies is a critical first step.

Going forward, an important policy imperative is developing data sharing platforms across local providers and organisations, which can be used to provide actionable and real time information on gaps in the supply and demand of skills to reduce potential skills shortages. By sharing information across organisations, employment, skills, and economic development actors can ensure they are successfully meeting the hiring needs of employers, which are a critical source of job creation. Box 4.2 provide a comprehensive example from the State of Michigan in the United States of local actors sharing information to better respond to the hiring needs of employers.

Box 4.2. **Workforce Intelligence Network in Michigan, United States**

WIN provides opportunities for co-ordination, efficiencies, and innovation across partners, by delivering real-time, actionable marketplace intelligence to support better, more efficient solutions for employers. This information helps consortium members, particularly community colleges, make better "real time" decisions regarding skill gaps. One of the tools used by WIN is a methodology to search the internet for job openings and resumes. This information, combined with data from the state's labor market information and special surveys, are incorporated in strategic plans and operational decisions. For example, SEMCA has been able to act upon this focused information and is currently working to create a talent pool for Computerized Numerical Control (CNC) and Welding. SEMCA also relies on WIN for detailed analysis of specific industries and occupations. Each year it completes a "Region Top Jobs" report, which includes the availability of current and projected opportunities by occupation, with the number of openings, and the rates of pay.

Within the advanced manufacturing sector, WIN connects with various organisations and associations and is leading important initiatives to better align the talent system with

Box 4.2. **Workforce Intelligence Network in Michigan, United States** *(cont.)*

talent needs. WIN serves as project lead and fiscal agent for InnoState, a new coalition among WIN, the Detroit Regional Chamber's Connection Point, the Michigan Manufacturing Technology Center (MMTC), the National Center for Manufacturing Sciences (NCMS), the Business Accelerators of Southeast Michigan (BANSEM) and the Society of Manufacturing Engineers (SME). Backed by funding from the Michigan Economic Development Corporation and various federal government agencies, InnoState is focused on expanding the New Product Contract Manufacturing Cluster of firms to increase their business and compete globally. WIN also convenes the skilled trades taskforce, which addresses employer talent needs through ongoing dialogue between the talent system and employers looking for skilled trades talent.

In the area of information technology, which is one of the fastest growing sectors in the region, WIN's cluster strategy includes the convening of an employer-led, multi-industry council, which has come to be known as the Tech Council of Southeast Michigan. The Council is convened to raise awareness of and shape community responses to regional talent needs. This group meets routinely and has two primary focuses:

- talent attraction and development; and
- marketing and branding Southeast Michigan as a technology hub.

The Council is comprised of more than 30 employers who have a significant need for information technology talent and is open to any additional company who may be interested in participating. WIN is directly involved with company-led training initiatives like "IT in the D" and serves as a communication conduit for the region's various talent partners. WIN is also working closely with the Michigan Economic Development Corporation, the state of Michigan, business accelerators, and many others to collaborate and help drive their efforts and programs aimed at closing the IT talent gap in Southeast Michigan.

Source: OECD (2014e), *Employment and Skills Strategies in the United States*, OECD Reviews on Local Job Creation, OECD Publishing.

Adding value through skills

Recommendation: Proceed with the reform of the apprenticeship system to make it a more attractive vocational educational pathway and foster more opportunities for work-based training.

The current apprenticeship system in Flanders – based on a "waterfall" model does not provide good training opportunities and is undervalued by both employers and youth. Going forward, it is important that the government examine what changes need to be made to the model to strengthen its attractiveness and ensure it is providing adequate work-based training opportunities, which are linked to quality jobs. A review process should be undertaken to look at its quality and relevance. It should consider expanding the model beyond traditional sectors as well as how to get employers more involved in its implementation and design.

Across the OECD, policy makers are focusing on the importance of providing good quality apprenticeship opportunities as a way of developing skills, which are well connected to the workplace. The benefit of a strong apprenticeship system is that employers become more engaged in articulating their skill needs and ensuring that the skills being developed align with their industry needs. Furthermore, within the OECD, there is a general consensus that apprenticeships can ease school to work transitions and lead to better labour market outcomes (Quintini and Manfredi, 2009). The challenge is that many young people still view apprenticeship opportunities as unattractive despite the availability of a high number of well-paying jobs.

In Ontario, Canada, a College of Trades was recently introduced, which is an employer-led body, that advises the government on technical provisions, overall curriculum, as well as policies and regulations. In 2009, legislation was passed to create the College. As an independent, industry-driven body, the College of Trades is designed to raise the profile of the skilled trades. The governance structure of the College includes a diverse range of employer and union representation. It is designed to make the system of apprenticeship training more responsive to the evolving skills and training needs of Ontario employers and consumers (Ontario College of Trades, 2011).

The Ontario government is committed to transforming the delivery of apprenticeship programmes by employing back-to-back education modules, blended and online learning to reduce the time apprentices are away from the workplace and accommodate employer workload priorities, resulting in improved apprenticeship completion. The Ontario government is also looking at enabling apprentices to complete portions of their workplace hours by expanding the in-school component to include real world, living lab work experiences and co-op placements.

Boxes 4.3 and 4.4 provide examples and lessons from apprenticeship programme experiences in the United States and Germany, which may be useful for Flanders in the further development of dual education opportunities.

Box 4.3. **Apprenticeship 2000 Programme, United States**

The goal of the Apprenticeship 2000 programme is to offer high school students opportunities in technical career fields and employment after graduation. Recognising the need for trained craftsmen, Blum Inc., along with Daetwyler Corporation in 1995, established the Apprenticeship 2000 programme in an effort to train their own workforce. After graduation from the programme, students can earn upwards of $34 000 per year in their selected career fields.

The Apprenticeship 2000 programme is an 8 000 hour program that spans four years of training. Upon graduation, students earn an AAS degree in Manufacturing Technology, and a Journeymans Certificate awarded by the state of North Carolina. At graduation, each apprentice will have invested approximately 6 400 hours inside one of the six sponsorship companies. The supplemental company instruction reinforces the student's classroom training by taking the classroom examples into real life situations. At Blum, company training is broken into three distinctive categories, each with their own sub categories. The three main categories are: Section One – Basic metal working/ bench work, Section Two – Machining (mill, lathe, CNC) and Section Three – Specialisation.

By training young people in basic machining, applications of engineering, and maintenance, Blum technicians become highly skilled to meet the needs of industry. Graduates of these technical career fields, offered by Apprenticeship 2000, have the ability to design, machine, document, and assemble changes virtually on demand. This makes each person and the company much more flexible to changes in trends, market conditions, and machine performance.

Source: Apprenticeship 2000, available at *http://apprenticeship2000.com/*.

Box 4.4. Lessons from Germany's Apprenticeship System

Previous OECD work has looked at the German apprenticeship model and identified the following key lessons for other countries in the development of an effective system:

A more transparent, simpler transition for young people

- Make the apprenticeship route an attractive option for good school performers but also ensure entry mechanisms for weaker school performers.
- Ensure schools have good links with firms and further training and tertiary education institutions, alongside strong career guidance.
- Pre-apprenticeship courses can serve as means to better prepare young people for a vocational route and to integrate more young people from disadvantaged backgrounds into apprenticeships.
- Training contracts can be offered to each school leaver with the necessary general skills and who is seeking an apprenticeship. Those not offered an in-company apprenticeship should be offered an recognised alternative by an external provider.

Access to career advancement training

- Supplement initial vocational training with advancement training to enable apprentices to progress to higher level jobs. In addition to specific occupational courses, general components could be included in this training, such as business administration and apprenticeship pedagogy.
- It is critical that advancement courses are certified and fit into national qualification frameworks so that apprentices who complete them can widen their professional prospects and are more mobile in the internal and external labour market.

Broad apprenticeship occupations

- Broader apprenticeship occupations mean more mobility and flexibility for apprentices. They also ensure more transferable skills, meaning workers are less vulnerable to unemployment in the face of an economic slowdown.
- Provide a mix of training for apprentices in joint core competences (such as teamwork) and occupation-specific competences.

Commitment to providing training and safeguarding apprenticeships

- An effective apprenticeship system is dependent on employers being committed to providing training. Agreements between the key social partners at all government levels can be crucial in re-engaging employers, particularly as more seek to reduce training costs following the economic crisis.
- Training pacts at the national, regional and local level can be a good way to ensure involvement by social partners and strong employer representation (e.g. via employers' associations, chambers of commerce, as well as unions and government). These do not necessarily require additional financing.
- Put in place mechanisms to keep apprentices on in times of high unemployment and to provide employment after completion, if even for a limited duration.

Source: Evans, S. and G. Bosch (2012), "Apprenticeships in London: Boosting Skills in a City Economy – With Comment on Lessons from Germany", *OECD Local Economic and Employment Development (LEED) Working Papers*, No. 2012/08, OECD Publishing, *http://dx.doi.org/10.1787/5k9b9mjcxp35-en*.

The government in Flanders could also look at how best to involve employers and vocational education institutions in the development of career pathway approaches, which provide a clear route from secondary school to training and then employment. Generally, pathways approaches are an articulation of knowledge, skills, and competencies and connecting education and work in a set of occupations that move from entry level to more complex positions. Career pathway programmes and initiatives can also have a specific emphasis on low skilled, unemployed or other target populations.

Career pathways approaches are used intensively in the United States and usually involve a partnership between vocational education institutions, secondary schools, employment services, economic development agencies, employers, unions, and other social services providers. The Department of Labour in the United States has played an advocacy role in promoting career pathway approaches as way of filling the need for a better trained workforce. Within the State of Oregon, more than 250 career pathway roadmaps have been created across 17 community colleges (Hamilton, 2012). Pennsylvania has previously used a career pathway model to develop a training programme targeted with the advanced manufacturing sector (see Box 4.5).

Box 4.5. **Career pathways/cluster approaches in the United States**

Maryland career sectors/clusters: Maryland started working on career sectors/career clusters in 1995 under the School to Work Opportunities Act. Within each county, there is both a Cluster Advisory Board (CAB), and an affiliate for each industry cluster. In Montgomery County, for example, where there is the third largest bio-technology cluster in the United States, they have a CAB is focused on the Biosciences, Health Science and Medicine cluster. The career cluster framework in Maryland is now embedded with flexible pathways. Students are required to take rigorous programmes, and although there are "vocational programmes" in the pathway, students are not short changed in general education.

Administrators, counselors, and faculty members are using the career cluster system to develop programs that extend from high school to two-and four-year colleges/universities, graduate schools, apprenticeship programs and the workplace. Although the cluster framework was originally developed for high schools and young people, it is now being adopted by Workforce Investment Boards and other programs serving adults.

Pennsylvania Mechatronics Partnerships: The Workforce Investment Boards (WIBs) of Berks and Lancaster counties in Pennsylvania, United States collaborated to develop the Industrial Maintenance and Mechatronics Industry Partnership of Pennsylvania, also known as the "Mechatronics Partnership". The region is home to a large base of manufacturing companies. Leading clusters include food manufacturing, wood products and a snack food cluster. Local manufacturers have long faced major challenge in finding skilled workers. Under this programme, local education and training providers collaborate with industry to create training programmes that begin in high school and which can lead to certification through two and four year degrees.

The Mechatronics Partnership has led to a number of positive outcomes, including preparing individuals for a variety of career paths by equipping them with a hybrid mix of skills that are easily transferable. Firms have benefitted from individuals with new mechatronics-related competencies who have introduced new ideas and approaches to the factory floor.

Box 4.5. **Career pathways/cluster approaches in the United States** *(cont.)*

The state has supported more than 80 such partnerships across Pennsylvania, engaging more than 6 300 firms. A large portion of the partnerships operate in manufacturing sectors, but there are a number in other clusters, such as logistics or health care. These partnerships are funded through a mix of industry, federal and state investments. They are seen as an example of good practice in the United States and the model has been applied to other states.

Source: Hamilton, V. (2012), "Career Pathway and Cluster Skill Development: Promising Models from the United States", *OECD Local Economic and Employment Development (LEED) Working Papers*, No. 2012/14, OECD Publishing, *http://dx.doi.org/10.1787/5k94g1s6f7td-en*.

Recommendation: Promote stronger engagement with employers in the design and implementation of employment and training programmes to create a culture of lifelong learning. Encourage network formation among employers who can take a lead role in the delivery of employment and skills policies.

Efforts to reduce skills mismatches and shortages require stronger engagement with employers in the facilitation of workplace training opportunities. While there are good examples of collaboration through the sectoral training funds, more can be done to articulate the benefits of training to employers and alert them to the opportunities available through these programmes. Employers complain about work readiness of young people and have high expectations of recruits. The Flemish government should continue to seek ways to develop an employer vision of responsibility to provide lifelong learning opportunities, particularly for lower-skilled individuals who lack access to workplace training opportunities.

The Talent Houses in Antwerp could be given the mandate to look at these policy issues and take a stronger leadership role in promoting workplace training opportunities across employers within their sector. Networking among employers at the local level is critical to leverage resources and funding to stimulate up-skilling opportunities aligned with new areas of economic growth. Some sector bodies, such as retail, host a significant share of poor quality jobs; therefore, they are well-placed to promote a culture of lifelong learning, which can increase overall job quality and labour market outcomes.

In the United Kingdom, the government is currently piloting major changes to the skills funding regime in England through the Employer Ownership Pilot (EOP). This pilot is giving employers direct access to government subsidy for workforce training as opposed to the traditional arrangement whereby all government funding goes direct to colleges and training providers. This means that employers have a direct role in determining the content and delivery of training activities. The second round of the pilot is also testing out the development of new Industrial Partnerships – involving employers, unions and others – with a remit for taking "wider responsibility for skills development in a place or sector".

Sweden had an apprenticeship system with a poor reputation among employers, therefore, the government sought to create new innovative higher vocational education programmes that use industry representatives and involve a mandatory workplace training component. While somewhat similar to HBO programmes in Flanders, employers in Sweden are more fully involved in determining programme content and delivery (see Box 4.6).

Another issue in Flanders relates to how best to support small and medium-sized enterprises (SMEs). In many OECD countries, SMEs are the engines of job creation. However

Box 4.6. **Higher Vocational Education (Yrkeshögskolan) programmes**

In Sweden, Higher Vocational Education (Yrkeshögskolan) is a post-secondary form of education that combines theoretical and practical studies in close co-operation with employers and industry. Programmes are offered in specific fields where there is an explicit demand for competence. These programmes combine theory and practice and workplace training forms an integral part of their delivery. There are hundreds of programmes available across Sweden.

The largest number of programmes offered is in the field of Business Finance and Administration, along with Sales and Manufacturing Technology. Other prominent areas include IT, Hospitality and Tourism, Health Care and Agriculture. Tuition is free of charge and many students are eligible for financial aid from the Swedish National Board for Student Aid (CSN). In order to safeguard the flexibility of the system, programmes can only be given twice and are then automatically terminated. After graduating from an HVE programme, students are qualified to go straight into employment. Standards are set high in HVE programmes. Students are highly goal-oriented, looking to further themselves professionally.

Higher Vocational Education is delivered in co-operation between education providers and those employers and industries affected by the programme. All programmes therefore have a strong emphasis on workplace training. The reason this is a good practice relates to the level of involvement by employers and industry representatives who play a significant role in the planning of HVE programme and their course content. Employers and industry representatives contribute to and influence the programme content by taking part as lecturers, joining in projects, welcoming study visits and by offering work placements.

Source: OECD (2015, forthcoming), *Employment and Skills Strategies in Sweden*, OECD Reviews on Local Job Creation, OECD Publishing.

they often face different and unique barriers to accessing the employment and skills system. SMEs should be encouraged to provide more up-skilling opportunities to their staff and target them specifically at lower-skilled workers, as it is higher skilled workers who tend to participate in these training opportunities. As highlighted in a previous OECD review of SME policies in Flanders, a first and necessary step for further coaching and support in organising training and development in SMEs is increasing awareness of the importance of training and development for business success (De Vos and Williams, 2011). While there are a number of comprehensive programmes and supports available to SMEs in Flanders, a key issue relates to the lack of awareness of available government support as well as a general reluctance to participate in government programmes because of perceived administrative barriers.

Ireland has emphasised the importance of stimulating networks among SMEs to get them more involved in the employment and skills system (see Box 4.7). In Korea, there are active networks of SMEs that form sectoral associations. These sectoral associations are connected to the local training institutions and arrange training for individuals (OECD, 2014). However, similar to other OECD countries, the challenge with skills training in SMEs is that employers are reluctant to provide training to their employees because of potential worker turnover. To offset such concerns among SMEs, the Ministry of Employment and Labour supports SMEs with training subsidies. For example, SMEs can be reimbursed 100% of the expenses whereas for large firms the upper limit is 80%.

Box 4.7. **Promoting ICT through Skillsnet in Ireland**

Skillnets was established in 1999 to promote and facilitate workplace training and up-skilling by SMEs. It is the largest organisation supporting workplace training in Ireland. In 2011, it had 70 operational networks through which it trained over 40 000 people for a total expenditure of EUR 25 million. It is a state-funded, enterprise-led body that co-invests with enterprises, particularly SMEs, when they co-operate in networks to identify and deliver training suited to their workforces. A network of SMEs, which are mostly sectoral or regional, is guided by a steering group of the local enterprise representatives. The steering group gives strategic direction and guidance to a network manager who co-ordinates all operational activity leading to the delivery of an agreed training plan with learning interventions suited for the member company workforces. The national programme is co-ordinated by Skillnets Ltd., who contract with all networks and provide programme support and monitoring to ensure the delivery of agreed quantitative and qualitative target outputs.

In 2011, 30 of these networks were located in Dublin, but were predominantly sectoral networks with a national remit and company membership. 25% of all Skillnets member companies and 33% of trainees were Dublin-based. Three networks were specific to the South East region (Carlow Kilkenny Skillnet, South Tipperary Skillnet and Waterford Chamber Skillnet). While Skillnets has a national impact, its influence is largely confined to SMEs which account for 94% of its 10 000 member companies. Originally set up to cater exclusively for the employed, since 2010 Skillnets has a mandate to include the provision of training for jobseekers. This happens both in an integrated manner with jobseekers attending programmes with employees, and also by focusing exclusively on the needs of jobseekers through the provision of dedicated longer-term programmes (e.g. the Jobseeker Support Programme) which includes work placements. Skillnets launched a pilot training initiative, ManagementWorks, providing management training to the SME community with a key focus on owner-managers.

Source: OECD (2014f), *Employment and Skills Strategies in Ireland*, OECD Reviews on Local Job Creation, OECD Publishing, *http://dx.doi.org/10.1787/9789264207912-en*.

Recommendation: Ensure career guidance and information systems are well-targeted to youth and individuals who are unemployed or at-risk of adjustment to support labour force attachment, as well as career progression and advancement.

Individuals require good information and well-articulated pathways to make successful career and labour market transitions. An important aspect to support school to work transitions is ensuring that there is good career guidance for unemployed individuals and students to make labour market and training decisions. In particular for youth, counsellors can play an important role is working with students and parents to define career interests and point individuals towards good training opportunities, which will equip them with the skills they need for labour market success. Box 4.8 provides a good example from Korea, which enables individuals to explore various career opportunities in sectors with strong growth potential.

The impending closure of Ford Genk resulted in a multi-stakeholder approach in Limburg to prepare for the conversion of the region, resulting in the development of the Strategic Action Plan for Limburg. This initiative demonstrates the strong level of partnership working that exists in Flanders with the plan leading to a number of concrete actions designed to respond to the downsizing and negative impacts that it will bring to the local economy. Going forward, individuals impacted by this closure will need targeted

Box 4.8. **Career advice in Korea and Canada**

Korea Job World is an interactive vocational experience centre located in the city of Seongnam-si in the Gyeonggi-do province, providing career guidance to the public in general, and young people in particular. It consists of an 80 000 square metre, six-story building, offering visitors a unique opportunity to explore and experience various occupations and career opportunities in an interactive way. It is designed to help people obtain a realistic view about possible professional choices and prospects, and to give career advice based on individual interests and aptitude. Visitors are guided through three main halls: The World Hall, Job Experience Hall, and the Career Design Hall. In the World Hall, images and descriptions about typical occupations and their employment trends are provided, whereas in the Job Experience Hall (mainly aimed at children and youth) these can be experienced in realistic settings. Finally, in the Career Design Hall visitors can perform an animated test based on the information and experiences gathered from the other rooms, testing their occupational interests and aptitude and given career advice accordingly. Korea Job World was opened in August 2012 after a period of pilot operation, and now hosts around 3 000 visitors a day.

Hamilton Employment Crawl, Canada: Each year McMaster University, in conjunction with Hamilton employers and supported with labour market information from Workforce Planning Hamilton, organises tours of local companies. "Crawls" are organised by sectors and each crawl involves visiting five enterprises to hear directly from management and staff what is happening in their field as well as upcoming job opportunities. The tours are followed by a networking opportunity with employer participants at a reception hosted by the University ("Employment Crawl"). Recently, four crawls were offered focusing on areas identified by economic development as targeted growth areas for the city. The four fields were:

- Manufacturing/Clean Air and Technology
- Creative Industries and Communications
- Food Processing/Goods Movement and Transportation
- Life Science and Health Care

Source: OECD (2014c), *Employment and Skills Strategies in Korea*, OECD Reviews on Local Job Creation, OECD Publishing; Ministry of Employment and Labor (2012), *2012 Employment and Labor Policy in Korea*, Ministry of Employment and Labor, Republic of Korea, p. 43, available at: *www.moel.go.kr/english/data/130111_2012_Employment%20and%20Labor%20Policy.pdf*; OECD (2014b), *Employment and Skills Strategies in Canada*, OECD Reviews on Local Job Creation, OECD Publishing, *http://dx.doi.org/10.1787/9789264209374-en*.

programmes, which build their skills for new economic opportunities. Flanders could look at other OECD countries' efforts to respond to large size downsizes.

In the United States, Michigan Shifting Gears is a career-transition programme designed to help seasoned professionals from large corporations develop the skills and training to transition into small company work environments. Initiated by the state of Michigan, it responds to the downsizing of many large corporations in the state, the elimination of professional jobs, and the need to increase entrepreneurship in the state. This programme includes an assessment, comprehensive classroom training, mentorship, coaching, small business simulation and internship with a start-up within a three-month window. By the end of this training, individuals are transformed into more adaptable professionals with experiences, knowledge and skills that are desirable by small, growing and innovative companies.

Many OECD countries are focused on re-activating the unemployed following a downsizing through short-term training opportunities. This "work-first" approach (e.g.

focusing on the shortest route to employment) is important however, one challenge faced by individuals faced with structural adjustment is the lack of longer term training opportunities available, which could better improve their employment outcomes. For unemployed adults or those at-risk of a lay-off, employment and training systems can provide them with a "second chance" by providing longer-term skills development opportunities within new or growing sectors of the economy.

In Ontario, Canada, a skills development programmes (called Second Career Programme) is focused on long-term skills development opportunities to help individuals at risk of displacement transition into new jobs and industries. The objective of the programme is to provide laid-off workers and unemployed individuals with long-term skills training to help them find employment in occupations with demonstrable labour market prospects in Ontario. Those eligible to participate include individuals who have been laid off since 1 January 2005, are unemployed or working an interim job, and are choosing to retrain for a career that is in demand. Individuals are not required to be eligible for unemployment insurance in Canada. The programme provides financial support for tuition, books, travel and other expenses to help eligible workers participate in training programmes. Individuals are eligible to take college training programmes in a range of occupations ranging from plumbers and electricians to community and social service workers, and early childhood educators. Individuals may qualify for financial support of up to CAD 28 000 (OECD, 2014b).

Targeting policy to local employment sectors and investing in quality jobs

Recommendation: Stimulate overall productivity and job quality through policies which promote the better utilisation of skills. Encourage the Talent House to focus on working with employers to stimulate overall demand for skills to boost local growth and competiveness.

A key aspect of job quality is looking at how individuals are using their existing skills in the workplace. While it is a new area for public policy, skills utilisation approaches can ultimately stimulate overall job creation through greater innovation and productivity improvements. Instead of rapidly designing a training programmes to respond to employers reporting skills shortages, these approaches take a broader workforce development approach by looking at how an organisation is structured as well as the design of jobs within the workplace.

While there are some initiatives undertaken at the local level, particularly in the Limburg region, skills utilisation efforts are not comprehensively supported across Flanders. The Flemish government should encourage closer working with employers to stimulate demand side initiatives under a mantra of Corporate Social Responsibility, which recognises the public and private benefits of encouraging and promoting quality jobs.

The Talent Houses in Antwerp are working well to match skills to certain sectors; however, much of their focus is on supply side initiatives. There is an opportunity for them to shift some of their focus on how to stimulate the demand for skills, which would create higher quality jobs and thereby attract higher skilled people into the city and region, which has broader economic development benefits. The City of Antwerp could look at the Limburg region where there appears to be some interesting programmes, which have sought to improve the better utilisation of skills, such as Platform Care Limburg and practice labs for innovation work organisation. These initiatives also demonstrate the strong role that can be played by unions (e.g. the ACV union) in promoting better quality job opportunities for workers and the unemployed. Their involvement is crucial to ensuring that any productivity gains from increased employee discretion and problem-solving are passed back to workers in terms of raised salaries and improved working conditions.

Previous OECD research has highlighted the importance of not just building the supply of skills in a local economy but also ensuring that skills are effectively utilised by employers (Froy and Giguère, 2010; Froy, Giguère and Meghnagi, 2012). Skills demand and utilisation will also increase if existing firms are able to diversify, upgrade their product market strategies, and move towards more knowledge-intensive production processes. As companies move into higher value added product and service markets, the levels of skills that they require, and the extent to which they utilise skills, tends to increase. There are a number of tools that can be used to support better work organisation and skills utilisation in order to increase productivity while improving job quality (see Box 4.9).

Box 4.9. **What practices promote more effective skills utilisation?**

The Australian Workforce and Productivity Agency (now mainstreamed within the Department of Industry) has outlined the following types of initiatives designed to make the use of skills more effective:

- **Job redesign:** involves changing the role or description of a job so that the skills of the employee are put to better use. This can include teamwork and flexibility in job descriptions and work arrangements with colleagues.
- **Employee participation:** includes involving employees in discussion on business strategy, which aims to more effectively use employees' knowledge and experience.
- **Autonomy:** includes giving employees more freedom and autonomy to make decisions in how they perform their job.
- **Job rotation:** involves facilitating the learning of new skills by shifting employees into different jobs and positions within the company.
- **Skills audit** (training needs assessment): aims to identify the skills that employees currently have and identify which skills are most needed.
- **Multi-skilling:** is related to job rotation and involves training employees in multiple skill sets, which enables them to perform other tasks, which are not included in their job description.
- **Knowledge transfer:** these types of initiatives can include developing new skills and training that is related to work or working with experienced workers to develop mentorships opportunities for younger staff.

Source: Skills Australia (2012), *Better Use of Skills, Better Outcomes: A Research Report on Skills Utilisation in Australia*, *www.awpa.gov.au/publications/documents/Skills-utilisation-research-report-15-May-2012.pdf*.

The vocational education and training system in Flanders can also play a prominent role in working closer with employers to undertake applied research, which improves production and business performance processes. They can also be instrumental in helping local industries to better access and better utilise skills when they are fully embedded in local economies. In areas of traditional low-skills, low-wage employment, the role played by vocational training system colleges in stimulating innovation in the local economy would seem to be particularly important. This can help local companies tap into relevant supply chains and expand their export opportunities to existing and emerging markets across Europe and the globe. Flanders could look at interesting workforce development initiatives, which have been introduced in Australia and Korea (see Box 4.10) to stimulate better quality jobs.

Box 4.10. Improving work organisation in Australia and Korea

Skills Connect, Australia: Skills Connect is a new approach to integrate workforce development programmes and services and to make them widely accessible to businesses. It provides access to programmes and funding via a national network of advisers, who provide support and advise about workforce development issues. This includes workforce planning, as well as attracting, retaining and developing employees. The specific programmes include support for Australian apprentices, literacy, language and numeracy training and assistance with developing or improving the skills of employees. At this stage, the National Workforce Development Fund is the principal component of Skills Connect. This programme assists businesses to identify and address their current and future workforce development needs by subsidising the training of new and existing workers. So far, $700 million AUD has been allocated to this fund for the period 2011-12 to 2015-16.

Techno parks in Korea to boost business innovation within SMEs: Bucheon (which is a suburb west of the capital city of Seoul) has several techno-parks which are business incubation buildings that accommodate many SMEs. These centres aim at attracting firms and improving working conditions in order to create job opportunities. The Techno Parks provide services to enhance SMEs' business administration capabilities. When SMEs need to accelerate their scale of business activities, they need the detailed information and knowledge about finance, marketing and management. To support them, the Techno Parks provide services to enhance their business administration capabilities; for example, exploring overseas markets, operating show rooms, hosting Design Contests, and arranging international certification supports. As global marketing environments are changing rapidly, the Techno Parks run classes for CEOs to enhance their skills for business administration and decision making. Also, there are more specialised education programmes such as outplacement start-up education and seminars for technology protection.

Source: OECD (2014c), *Employment and Skills Strategies in Australia*, OECD Reviews on Local Job Creation, OECD Publishing, *http://dx.doi.org/10.1787/9789264207899-en*; OECD (2014d), *Employment and Skills Strategies in Korea*, OECD Reviews on Local Job Creation, OECD Publishing, *http://dx.doi.org/10.1787/9789264216563-en*.

Recommendation: Build stronger entrepreneurship skills for youth and adults to stimulate overall demand and job creation. This can be done by promoting entrepreneurship as a viable career option and providing comprehensive support and tools to individuals to help them start their own business.

Another critical level in stimulating job creation locally is creating a culture of entrepreneurship. This is particularly true for local areas which are experiencing structural adjustments, such as the Limburg region, where the Ford factory is set to close, resulting in significant direct and indirect job losses for the community.

Entrepreneurship skills can assist individuals in developing successful businesses and creating jobs. In particular, the vocational and higher education system should ensure that course curriculum includes an adequate focus on building these types of skills. For under-represented groups, previous OECD research has highlighted the benefits of encouraging entrepreneurship among these individuals to stimulate overall labour supply as well as job creation (OECD, 2013).

More can be done in Flanders to promote entrepreneurship as a viable career option for youth by giving them better support to start their own business. There is evidence that young people are enthusiastic about starting businesses (including non-profits) but they face greater barriers due to lower levels of skills, less experience, more difficulty accessing financing, and less developed business networks. More should be done to support the acquisition of entrepreneurship skills by youth by embedding entrepreneurship teaching throughout the education system, providing information, advice, coaching and mentoring, facilitating access to financing, and offering support infrastructure for business start-up.

Box 4.11. **Promoting Entrepreneurship following Structural Adjustment in Canada**

Entrepreneurial activity is seen as one of the keys to diversifying the local economy of Shawinigan. For many years, Shawinigan was an industrial town built around its large electric power facility and heavy industry. Industrialization brought steady well-paying work in forestry, aluminium production and textiles. The city became a victim of structural changes in the global economy with many employers shutting down their operations. With the impending closure of another enterprise in 2009, prominent people in the community were brought together to look at the future of city considering its strengths and weaknesses. Based on this collaboration, the city is pursuing an approach that looks to develop a community of entrepreneurs and small business operations as a sustainable economic base.

What is of particular interesting about this approach is the partnership of a number of different actors each guided by a different policy focus (e.g. economic development, education or employment) to implement a local horizontal approach. The mechanism for this integration was a small amount of funding directed to the municipality by a departing employer.

A Diversification Committee was established composed of key funding and government agencies. The committee realised that in order to be effective, they would have to create a common local plan that would inform their vertical accountabilities. Specific areas of collaboration have been the strategic use of non-governmental and governmental funding to maximize total grants. An entrepreneurial forum was created to:

- promote entrepreneurism as a career;
- increase the percentage of individuals choosing an entrepreneurial path;
- develop entrepreneurial attributes among the youth;
- grow synergies among organizations that develop the economy and community; and,
- recognize and emphasize initiative, creativity, solidarity and communal engagement.

In collaboration with the school commission, Shawinigan opened the entrepreneurship centre in 2013. It represents a unique project in the province of Québec positioned in that it is a tangible action brought about by the entrepreneurial forum with the collaboration of the Diversification Committee.

The entrepreneurship centre is located in an old textile factory which has been completely renovated. The city of Shawinigan advanced $3 million for the project with approximately $2 million coming from other sources. The entrepreneurship centre offers skills development programmes along with other supports that will allow the growth of a critical mass of entrepreneurs.

Source: OECD (2014b), *Employment and Skills Strategies* in Canada, OECD Reviews on Local Job Creation, OECD Publishing, *http://dx.doi.org/10.1787/9789264209374-en*.

Being inclusive

Recommendation: Strengthen linkages between the education system and employment, and training agencies to reduce youth drop-outs. Continue to target early-school leavers and provide follow-up support while examining ways of involving youth more in programme design and delivery.

To ensure that the supply of skills adequately meets labour market demand, it is important to strengthen the linkages between the education system and employment, and training agencies. Schools should work more closely with VDAB and the vocational education system to create clearer, simpler and more recognised pathways into training as well as the labour market. In particular, it is important that more out-reach is conducted by VDAB and other partners with secondary schools to ensure that youth at-risk can be identified early and adequate supports and interventions can be put in place to reduce early school leavers and the number of NEETs. At the local level, addressing youth unemployment is a clear policy priority in both Antwerp and Limburg. A number of comprehensive programmes and policies have been put in place, including a strategy to target early school leavers and provide them with work experience opportunities to develop long-term labour market attachment. Furthermore, there is a strong policy focus on improving transitions from school to work.

Efforts in this area must continue as previous OECD research has shown that youth who drop out of school early, having acquired no or few qualifications, are at particular risk of becoming permanently disconnected from the labour market (OECD, 2013). In the past, the higher availability of employment meant that those who had not completed compulsory education could pass easily into employment, albeit often poor quality and temporary, but the decreasing number of job openings has made this harder. To be most effective, policy makers need to improve mechanisms for identifying those at risk of dropping out, and prevent this from happening.

When young excluded people start work, it is important that follow-up support is provided to ensure they are gradually building basic employability skills. Providing on-going support and training once young people are in work to help them retain their employment and secure on-going career progression is also important (OECD, 2014b). This support will help ensure sustainable employment and the skills necessary to retain a job or re-enter the labour market if faced with a lay-off.

The development of employability skills through workplace training opportunities is an important component of the BladeRunners programme in Vancouver, Canada where youth receive health and safety training to help them build self-esteem and confidence. Support from programme co-ordinators is a key defining feature of this model (see Box 4.12). Off-the-job support takes many forms: referrals to various health, education and social services; financial support for obtaining stable housing; support in the form of public transport vouchers and meals; informal counselling about further training and education; and financial support for additional training programme fees. The underlying and fundamental goal of all support is to make sure that participants are able to be placed in jobs and to maintain stable employment and long-term attachment to the labour market.

The Ontario government in Canada has recently announced a new Youth Employment Strategy is its recent 2013 Budget. This strategy is designed to help more young people find jobs, while also ensuring the employers can hire the skilled workers they need in today's economy. The entire strategy is supported by a total investment of $295 million CDN over

Box 4.12. **BladeRunners, Canada**

BladeRunners is an employment programme that helps youth (ages 15-30) with multiple barriers to employment build careers in construction and other industries throughout the province of British Columbia, Canada. The ultimate goal of the program is to develop skills and work experience that foster long-term attachment to the labour force and to support the social and community integration of young people.

All Bladerunners programme participants are paired up with one of the BladeRunners co-ordinators. This is not done through an assignation process, but rather follows the preferences of participants and their choice to engage with one or another of the co-ordinators. Co-ordinators provide support directly if possible, or through their network of contacts in community organisations. Most programme co-ordinators have a history in the community and have often encountered in the past some of the same difficulties faced by BladeRunners participants. Prior to placement, all work equipment (hard hats, boots, rain gear, etc.) is paid for by the BladeRunners programme and participants are accompanied by a co-ordinator in order to make this purchase. Then, on the first day of work, a BladeRunners co-ordinator will bring the participant to the construction site and introduce him or her to the foreman, contractor or tradesperson, and to other BladeRunners if any are already working on the site. Over the subsequent days, the co-ordinator will return to the site to ensure that the contractor, the tradespeople and the BladeRunners participant are satisfied with the placement. If required, co-ordinators will refer participants to other social service providers, assist with housing and transport needs and counsel young people about further training and permanent job opportunities. Funds are available to help stabilise housing (first month's rent and damage deposit), for transport (bus tickets) and food (lunches on site, if needed) – this support is offered because it is deemed essential to ensure employability.

Support is offered whenever programme participants need it, on or off the job. It is available 24 hours a day, 7 days a week. BladeRunners participants all have the mobile phone number of "their" co-ordinator who can be reached at all times. Although emergency calls are rare, they do occur and co-ordinators are willing to provide any useful assistance at these times. In the past, access to support from co-ordinators was offered only up to 18 months after placement. However, in practice, programme co-ordinators always maintained an open-door policy and continued to engage with any past BladeRunners participants who expressed a need for support in returning to employment. Today, no time limits are placed on the availability of support.

Source: Travkina, Froy and Pyne (2013), "Local Strategies for Youth Employment: Learning from Practice", OECD *Local Economic and Employment Development* (LEED), available at *www.oecd.org/cfe/leed/Local%20Strategies%20for%20Youth%20Employment%20FINAL%20FINAL.pdf.*

two years, and is estimated to create 30 000 new job opportunities. The strategy focuses on jobs, entrepreneurship and innovation for youth in Ontario and includes new programmes, which provide hiring incentives to employers to offer young people in all regions of the province an entry point to long-term employment. An Ontario Youth Entrepreneurship Fund has also been set up to supports the next generation of entrepreneurs through mentorship, startup capital and outreach supports. Flanders could look to this strategy in further developing actions around tackling youth unemployment.

Flanders could also look at involving youth more in the delivery of youth employment programmes using a principle of co-design, where youth are actively involved in making a programme successful. This principle of co-design goes beyond an advisory role and directly involves youth in the delivery of the programme. For example, Sweden has recently introduced the Unga-In project, which takes an innovative approach to assisting youth by directing involving young people as staff (see Box 4.13). This helps to build credibility and ensure that at-risk youth can interact with role models, who can help to show them the benefits of a sustainable job.

Box 4.13. **Sweden: The Unga In Project**

Unga In (meaning young in) is a project to fight youth exclusion from the labour market. The project targets drop-outs who are not participating in employment or skills programmes. The goal of the project is to give young people greater ambition and motivation to participate in the labour market. The risk is that they would otherwise be permanently excluded, with consequences for themselves and for society in general.

The project is an outgrowth of a well-established organization called *Fryshuset*, after the storage house ("the freezing house") where they are located in Stockholm. *Fryshuset* was set up with the intention to provide a space for young people. *Fryshuset* is a partner in the project, together with the city of Stockholm and the organisation Friends, which runs programmes in schools to prevent social conflicts. The project *Unga In* is owned by Arbetsförmedlingen and co-funded by the European Social Fund.

Unga In provides basic services by Arbetsförmedlingen, to help youth find motivating education and job opportunities. What makes it different is how it approaches the target group through its outreach activities. Project staff are other young people and therefore can establish greater trust with the participants. Participants meet with staff in a "job garage" where there are provided with counselling and mentoring opportunities in a more informal setting.

Source: OECD (2015, forthcoming), *Employment and Skills Strategies in Sweden*, OECD Reviews on Local Job Creation, OECD Publishing, Paris.

References

Bogaerts, K. et al. (2011), "Building Flexibility and Accountability into Local Employment Services: Country Report for Belgium", *OECD Local Economic and Employment Development (LEED) Working Papers*, No. 2011/11, OECD Publishing, Paris, *http://dx.doi.org/10.1787/5kg3mkv0448s-en*.

Barr, J. et al. (2012), "Local Job Creation: How Employment and Training Agencies Can Help – The Labour Agency of the Autonomous Province of Trento, Italy", *OECD Local Economic and Employment Development (LEED) Working Papers*, No. 2012/17, OECD Publishing, Paris, *http://dx.doi.org/10.1787/5k919d0trlf6-en*.

Dean, A. (2013), "Tackling Long-Term Unemployment Amongst Vulnerable Groups", *OECD Local Economic and Employment Development (LEED) Working Papers*, No. 2013/11, OECD Publishing, Paris, *http://dx.doi.org/10.1787/5k43jct8n2nv-en*.

De Vos, A. and I. Williams (2011), "Leveraging Training Skills Development in SMEs: An Analysis of East Flanders, Belgium", *OECD Local Economic and Employment Development (LEED) Working Papers*, No. 2011/17, OECD Publishing, Paris, *http://dx.doi.org/10.1787/5kg0vsrqwhf5-en*.

Evans, S. and G. Bosch (2012), "Apprenticeships in London: Boosting Skills in a City Economy – With Comment on Lessons from Germany", *OECD Local Economic and Employment Development (LEED) Working Papers*, No. 2012/08, OECD Publishing, Paris, *http://dx.doi.org/10.1787/5k9b9mjcxp35-en*.

Hamilton, V. (2012), "Career Pathway and Cluster Skill Development: Promising Models from the United States", *OECD Local Economic and Employment Development (LEED) Working Papers*, No. 2012/14, OECD Publishing, Paris, *http://dx.doi.org/10.1787/5k94g1s6f7td-en*.

OECD/The European Commission (2013), *The Missing Entrepreneurs: Policies for Inclusive Entrepreneurship in Europe*, OECD Publishing, Paris, *http://dx.doi.org/10.1787/9789264188167-en*.

OECD (2015, forthcoming), *Employment and Skills Strategies in Sweden*, OECD Reviews on Local Job Creation, OECD Publishing, Paris.

OECD (2014a), *Employment and Skills Strategies in the Czech Republic*, OECD Reviews on Local Job Creation, OECD Publishing, Paris, *http://dx.doi.org/10.1787/9789264208957-en*.

OECD (2014b), *Employment and Skills Strategies in Canada*, OECD Reviews on Local Job Creation, OECD Publishing, Paris, *http://dx.doi.org/10.1787/9789264209374-en*.

OECD (2014c), *Employment and Skills Strategies in Australia*, OECD Reviews on Local Job Creation, OECD Publishing, Paris, *http://dx.doi.org/10.1787/9789264207899-en*.

OECD (2014d), *Employment and Skills Strategies in Korea*, OECD Reviews on Local Job Creation, OECD Publishing, Paris, *http://dx.doi.org/10.1787/9789264216563-en*.

OECD (2014e), *Employment and Skills Strategies in the United States*, OECD Reviews on Local Job Creation, OECD Publishing, Paris, *http://dx.doi.org/10.1787/9789264209398-en*.

OECD (2014f), *Employment and Skills Strategies in Ireland*, OECD Reviews on Local Job Creation, OECD Publishing, Paris, *http://dx.doi.org/10.1787/9789264207912-en*.

Ministry of Employment and Labor (2012), *2012 Employment and Labor Policy in Korea*, Ministry of Employment and Labor, Republic of Korea, p. 43, available at: *www.moel.go.kr/english/data/130111_2012_Employment%20and%20Labor%20Policy.pdf*.

Quintini, G. and T. Manfredi (2009), "Going Separate Ways? School-to-Work Transitions in the United States and Europe", *OECD Social, Employment and Migration Working Papers*, No. 90, OECD Publishing, Paris, *http://dx.doi.org/10.1787/221717700447*.

Travkina, Froy and Pyne (2013), *Local Strategies for Youth Employment: Learning from Practice*, OECD Local Economic and Employment Development (LEED), available at *www.oecd.org/cfe/leed/Local%20Strategies%20for%20Youth%20Employment%20FINAL%20FINAL.pdf*.

ORGANISATION FOR ECONOMIC CO-OPERATION AND DEVELOPMENT

The OECD is a unique forum where governments work together to address the economic, social and environmental challenges of globalisation. The OECD is also at the forefront of efforts to understand and to help governments respond to new developments and concerns, such as corporate governance, the information economy and the challenges of an ageing population. The Organisation provides a setting where governments can compare policy experiences, seek answers to common problems, identify good practice and work to co-ordinate domestic and international policies.

The OECD member countries are: Australia, Austria, Belgium, Canada, Chile, the Czech Republic, Denmark, Estonia, Finland, France, Germany, Greece, Hungary, Iceland, Ireland, Israel, Italy, Japan, Korea, Luxembourg, Mexico, the Netherlands, New Zealand, Norway, Poland, Portugal, the Slovak Republic, Slovenia, Spain, Sweden, Switzerland, Turkey, the United Kingdom and the United States. The European Union takes part in the work of the OECD.

OECD Publishing disseminates widely the results of the Organisation's statistics gathering and research on economic, social and environmental issues, as well as the conventions, guidelines and standards agreed by its members.

LOCAL ECONOMIC AND EMPLOYMENT DEVELOPMENT (LEED)

The OECD Programme on Local Economic and Employment Development (LEED) has advised governments and communities since 1982 on how to respond to economic change and tackle complex problems in a fast-changing world. Its mission is to contribute to the creation of more and better quality jobs through more effective policy implementation, innovative practices, stronger capacities and integrated strategies at the local level. LEED draws on a comparative analysis of experience from the five continents in fostering economic growth, employment and inclusion. For more information on the LEED Programme, please visit *www.oecd.org/cfe/leed*.

OECD PUBLISHING, 2, rue André-Pascal, 75775 PARIS CEDEX 16
(84 2015 03 1 P) ISBN 978-92-64-22798-9 – 2015-01

www.ingramcontent.com/pod-product-compliance
Lightning Source LLC
LaVergne TN
LVHW081420110826
845149LV00010B/1811
9789264227989